TAHITI AND BORA BORA TRAVEL GUIDE

Exploring the Natural Wonders of
Tahiti and Bora BoraTitle. Exploring
Paradise in the South Pacific

By
Jodi M. wyatt

Table of Contents

Preface

I was immediately mesmerized by the gorgeous beaches of Tahiti and Bora Bora when I first set foot on them. The South Pacific sun's warm embrace, the glistening turquoise waves, and the swaying palm trees combined to produce a sensory symphony that awoke my spirit and left an enduring impression on my soul. Then I understood I had discovered something genuinely extraordinary—a paradise that words alone could not adequately describe.

I couldn't help but feel driven to tell others about this unmatched experience as I explored the islands in greater depth, becoming immersed in local culture and discovering the hidden gems that waiting around every turn. I wanted to capture the spirit of Tahiti and Bora Bora, reveal its secrets, and provide other travelers a guide that will improve their own trip to these idyllic locales.

This book, "Tahiti and Bora Bora Travel Guide: Exploring Paradise in the South Pacific," is the outcome of that goal. It is a labor of love that resulted from my love of travel, adventure, and the quest to find the most amazing places on earth. It is my honest hope that you will find motivation, helpful suggestions, and an invitation to set out on your own individual voyage through Tahiti and Bora Bora inside these pages.

I have devoted my entire being to compiling a thorough guide that covers the highlights and undiscovered gems of these islands. I've tried to give you a road map to the treasures that await you in this part of the world, from the vibrant marketplaces of Papeete to the opulent overwater villas of Bora Bora.

Beyond the logistics of travel, this book is also a celebration of the South Pacific's spirit—the friendliness of its people, the depth of its culture, and the breathtaking natural beauty that is all around you. The manner of life of the

Polynesians, their close ties to the land and the water, and the legends that have been passed down through the generations are all explored in this book.

I urge you to embark on this voyage with an open heart and mind as you flip through the pages and devise your own adventure. Allow yourself to become engrossed in the hues, aromas, and sounds of Tahiti and Bora Bora, and let their seduction sweep you away. Accept the unanticipated and accept the aloha attitude that permeates every aspect of life here.

I am honored and grateful to be your captain on this amazing journey. May you use this book as a compass, a source of inspiration, and a traveling companion while you explore Tahiti and Bora Bora's treasures. May it allow you to make lifelong memories and change you forever with the magic of this tropical paradise.

So come along with me as we set out on this incredible adventure, my traveler. Let's explore

Tahiti and Bora Bora; may these pages serve as a gateway to the awaited paradise. Happy travels!

Introduction

Welcome to Tahiti and Bora Bora, two enthralling islands where the beautiful setting of dreams is created by blue oceans, white sand beaches, and lush tropical scenery. This travel book is your ticket to an incredible tour through the most sought-after locations in the South Pacific, where you'll experience the true meaning of paradise.

We cordially invite you to travel virtually to Tahiti and Bora Bora in this book, two of French Polynesia's crowning achievements. These islands provide a stunning fusion of natural beauty, colorful culture, and a tranquil environment that will leave you spellbound, whether you're planning a romantic honeymoon, a family trip, or a solitary excursion.

Our intention is to give you a thorough and educational travel guide that will be a reliable travel companion as you explore Tahiti and Bora

Bora. Making the most of your time in this tropical paradise requires a variety of useful advice, insider knowledge, and must-see attractions, all of which we've carefully selected for you.

We shall delve into Tahiti and Bora Bora's essence chapter by chapter, learning about their special charms and undiscovered gems. We'll lead you through the vibrant local markets, historic Polynesian temples, exhilarating water sports, and opulent resorts that make these islands a veritable paradise on Earth, from the humming capital city of Papeete to the remote beaches of Bora Bora.

You'll learn about the Polynesian people's rich cultural past, friendly hospitality, and close ties to the land and water with each page you turn. Enjoy the mouthwatering flavors of regional cuisine, take part in traditional dances, and discover the stories and legends that have shaped the history of the islands.

Tahiti and Bora Bora have something to offer everyone, whether you're an adventurer hoping to explore colorful coral reefs, a leisure enthusiast looking for a quiet beachside getaway, or a cultural traveler keen to learn about the customs of the South Pacific.

Pack your luggage, get your camera packed, and get ready for an incredible voyage across Tahiti and Bora Bora's gorgeous oceans, palm-fringed shores, and vibrant culture. This travel manual is your key to discovering these paradisiacal islands' mysteries and making sure that your vacation is not only amazing but also seamless and full of wonder.

Are you prepared to let Bora Bora and Tahiti enchant you? Let's start off on this road together!

Welcome

Welcome to Tahiti and Bora Bora, two beautiful islands where paradise is a reality. As we explore the beauty, culture, and adventure that await you in these tropical havens, be ready to embark on a journey of a lifetime.

Papeete, the bustling capital of Tahiti, the largest island in French Polynesia, beckons you. Explore the crowded markets that are stocked with handicrafts, unique fruits, and flavorful spices. Take in the rich hues and flavors of the regional cuisine, which ranges from mouthwatering fresh seafood dishes to the cherished poisson cru. Witness the captivating dances that depict the rich history of the island while listening to the throbbing beats of Tahitian music.

We focused on Bora Bora, a location that need no introduction, after leaving Tahiti. The overwater bungalows and famous turquoise lagoon of Bora Bora, known as the pinnacle of luxury and natural beauty, have won over tourists from all over the world. Here, you'll find a paradise for people who enjoy water sports, from snorkeling amid colorful coral reefs to scuba diving in the Pacific Ocean. In the shadow of Mount Otemanu, indulge in luxurious spa services, unwind on gorgeous beaches, and relish delectable cuisine.

However, Tahiti and Bora Bora's appeal goes far beyond their well-known attractions. Numerous smaller, isolated islets, each with a special appeal, surround these islands. The sacred island of Raiatea, which is also the cradle of Polynesian culture, provides a window into the past. Explore Huahine's verdant landscapes and take in its intriguing history. The aromatic plantations of Taha'a, sometimes known as the "Vanilla Island," promise to provide sensual pleasures.

To help you make the most of your time in Tahiti and Bora Bora, we will assist you traverse the must-see sights, offer insider knowledge, and offer useful recommendations throughout this travel guide. These islands have something to offer any traveler, whether they are looking for adventure, relaxation, cultural immersion, or a combination of all three.

So get ready to give in to Tahiti and Bora Bora's charm. Let the warm friendliness of the Polynesian people, the glistening waves, and the swaying of the palm palms embrace you. Allow yourself to be enchanted by the beauty of these islands, where paradise becomes your home away from home and dreams become reality.

Welcome to Tahiti and Bora Bora; the adventure has just begun.

About French Polynesia

The French Polynesian Islands are a French overseas territory in the South Pacific Ocean. Over five archipelagos, it is made up of 118 islands and atolls; Tahiti and Bora Bora are two of its most well-known resort areas.

French Polynesia's largest and most populated island, Tahiti, is frequently referred to as the "Queen of the Pacific." It functions as the regional center for politics, business, and culture. On Tahiti's northwest coast, Papeete, the capital city, is a bustling metropolis with a blend of modern conveniences and traditional Polynesian charm.

On the other hand, the little island of Bora Bora, which sits northwest of Tahiti, is well known for its magnificent natural beauty. It is famous for its recognizable blue lagoon, beautiful tropical scenery, and opulent overwater bungalows that draw honeymooners, famous people, and tourists looking for a dream vacation.

The entirety of French Polynesia is famed for its immaculate white sand beaches, clean lagoons, and abundant marine life. It is a mecca for adventure lovers because it provides a variety of outdoor activities like snorkeling, scuba diving, sailing, and surfing.

The islands of French Polynesia are home to a rich Polynesian culture. Throughout the archipelago, one can observe the traditional practices, language, music, dance, and artistic expression of the Polynesian people. Visitors have the chance to fully immerse themselves in the rich cultural legacy of the area, from historic marae (holy sites) to spellbinding traditional performances.

The cuisine of French Polynesia is a combination of Polynesian, French, and outside influences. Visitors will enjoy the excellent gastronomic experience offered by the native cuisine, which is dominated by fresh seafood, tropical fruits, and distinctive flavors.

Remember that French Polynesia lives at a slower pace known as "island time," which enables visitors to unwind and enjoy the serene atmosphere that permeates the archipelago.

French Polynesia offers a mesmerizing fusion of unmatched natural beauty, cultural diversity, and life-changing experiences, whether you decide to explore the vibrant markets of Papeete, take in the natural beauties of Bora Bora, or travel off the beaten road to less well-known islands. It is a place that catches people's attention and makes a lasting impression on those who are fortunate enough to go there.

Brief History

Brief History of Bora Bora and Tahiti:
Both the French Polynesian islands of Tahiti and Bora Bora have a long and rich history. A quick synopsis of their pasts is given below:

Tahiti: Tahiti is significant because it is the political and cultural hub of French Polynesia. Around 1,500 years ago, Polynesians arrived and established a colony there. Their offspring, the Ma'ohi, later developed a complex society with a hierarchical system. Tahiti was split up into chiefdoms that were commanded by strongmen.

Samuel Wallis, a British adventurer, was the first European to travel to Tahiti in 1767. Louis Antoine de Bougainville, a French explorer, arrived soon after. Captain James Cook followed in 1769. Tahitian society underwent considerable changes as a result of European contact, including the spread of alien diseases and the influence of Christian missionaries.

In 1842, Tahiti was designated as a French protectorate, and a French colony was established there in 1880. The island was a significant American military outpost during World War II.

More recently, in 1984, Tahiti obtained internal autonomy within the French Republic, and in 2004, when French Polynesia was established as an overseas collectivity, Tahiti received more political independence.

Northwest of Tahiti is the island of Bora Bora, which has a rich past of its own. Like Tahiti, the island was populated by Polynesians in the fourth century AD, and local leaders oversaw its administration.

Dutch explorer Jakob Roggeveen made touch with Bora Bora for the first time in 1722. Before James Cook, a British navigator, arrived in 1769, the island remained largely uninhabited. With the creation of Catholic and Protestant missions in the 19th century, European influence grew over time.

Together with the rest of French Polynesia, Bora Bora was made a protectorate of France in 1842. As a station for American military supplies during World War II, the island played a strategic role.

The magnificent natural beauty and opulent resorts of Bora Bora have made it a well-known tourist destination in recent times.

While also incorporating contemporary influences, Tahiti and Bora Bora both maintain a strong commitment to their Polynesian history. They are now cherished tourist spots that provide tourists with a singular fusion of history, culture, and breathtaking vistas.

How to Get There and Around

Travel to Tahiti and Bora Bora requires both air and water travel, as does getting about the islands. An overview of traveling in and around Tahiti and Bora Bora is provided below:

How to Get to Tahiti: 1. By Air: Fa'a' International Airport (PPT) in Papeete, Tahiti, is the main entry point for French Polynesia. International planes land there from significant cities all around the world. Tahiti is serviced by a number of airlines, including Air Tahiti Nui, French Bee, Air France, and United Airlines.

How to go from Tahiti to Bora Bora: 1. By Air: Domestic flights are the most popular method of travel. Regular flights are run by Air Tahiti between Bora Bora Airport (BOB) and Tahiti's Faa'a Airport (PPT). 50 minutes or such is the average flight time.

2. By Ferry: Another option is to go from Tahiti to Bora Bora by ferry. Aremiti runs the boat service, which travels for around four hours and provides beautiful vistas of the nearby islands.

Using a car to get around Tahiti is a practical method to see the island. There are car rental companies in major cities and at the airport. The roads on the island are in good condition, and driving is done on the right.

2. By Taxi: Taxis are easily accessible in Tahiti, especially in Papeete and at the airport. It is wise to haggle over the fare before setting out on the voyage.

3.By Bus: Tahiti's Le Truck is a well-liked mode of public transportation. These vibrant open-air buses run along predetermined routes and provide an inexpensive means of getting across the island. They do, however, follow a strict schedule, so it's crucial to verify the timetables beforehand.

1. By Boat: Since Bora Bora is a very tiny island, boats are the primary form of transportation. Shuttle services are offered frequently by hotels and resorts between the airport and lodging. For traveling to adjacent motus (small islets) or for exploring the lagoon, water taxis and private boat rentals are also offered.

2. On a Bike: Bora Bora is known for its bike-friendly roads, so exploring the island on a bike can be a relaxing way to do it. Guest bicycles are frequently provided at resorts.

3. By Taxi: You can take a taxi in Bora Bora for both quick journeys and island tours. It is wise to haggle over the fare in advance.

French Polynesia's smaller islands and atolls can sometimes only be reached by domestic flights or boat transfers. Inter-island flights are run by Air Tahiti between several islands and archipelagos.

The South Pacific's breathtaking scenery can be experienced while traveling between the French Polynesian islands, whether by air or boat.

The Heart of French Polynesia "Tahiti".

Tahiti, sometimes known as "The Heart of French Polynesia," has a unique position within the archipelago. Tahiti, the biggest and most populous island in French Polynesia, is the region's commercial, political, and cultural hub. With its bright energy, breathtaking vistas, and rich Polynesian heritage, it perfectly encapsulates the spirit of the South Pacific.

Tahiti Nui (Big Tahiti) and Tahiti Iti (Small Tahiti) are the two main regions of the island of Tahiti. Tahiti Iti is a less populated and more untamed region noted for its breathtaking natural beauty, whereas Tahiti Nui, which is the greater half, is where the capital city of Papeete is located.

The vibrant capital and entryway to the rest of French Polynesia is Papeete, which is situated on the island of Tahiti Nui's northwest coast. It presents a colorful fusion of contemporary elements and traditional Polynesian culture. The marketplaces here are bright and loaded with crafts, colorful textiles, and tropical fruits. The "Papeete Harbor Front," a waterfront promenade, is a well-liked location to stroll, take in the ocean views, and eat at waterfront eateries.

Tahiti is well known for its stunning scenery. Towering volcanic peaks, including Mount Orohena, French Polynesia's highest peak, dominate the island. Tahiti is a haven for hikers and nature enthusiasts thanks to its verdant valleys, flowing waterfalls, and lush tropical woods.

Tahiti is a vibrant center of Polynesian culture, and tourists can fully experience this ancient legacy there. You can learn about customs and rituals from the island's many cultural landmarks, such as marae (old stone temples). Intriguing performances known as "heiva" events feature the colorful music and dance of Tahiti, with its throbbing drumbeats and beautiful motions.

Tahiti also has a huge selection of experiences and activities. You may explore the island's surrounding coral reefs and abundant marine life via snorkeling, scuba diving, and deep-sea fishing. The renowned Teahupo'o break offers world-class surfing opportunities. And Tahiti's gorgeous beaches and five-star resorts provide a haven of peace and pampering for visitors seeking leisure.

The natural splendor, gracious people, and lively cultural traditions of Tahiti fully capture the essence of French Polynesia. Tahiti welcomes you to experience the heart and spirit of this island paradise, whether you're strolling through the bustling streets of Papeete, trekking through verdant valleys, or soaking up the sun on a remote beach.

Overview of Tahiti

The largest and most populated island in French Polynesia, Tahiti, is a captivating travel destination that provides the ideal balance of scenic beauty, cultural diversity, and contemporary conveniences. An idea of things to anticipate when traveling to Tahiti is given below:

The capital of French Polynesia, Papeete, is situated on Tahiti's northwest coast and is known for being a vibrant city. With bustling marketplaces, a thriving nightlife, and a blend of French and Polynesian elements, it acts as the island's political and economic hub.

2. Awe-inspiring Natural Wonders: Tahiti is known for its stunning scenery. Mount Orohena,

one of the island's many green summits, offers breathtaking 360-degree vistas. For those who enjoy the outdoors and the great outdoors, a paradise is created by lush valleys, tumbling waterfalls, and immaculate beaches.

3. Polynesian Culture: Tahiti preserves its extensive Polynesian tradition, giving visitors the chance to fully experience the indigenous way of life. Investigate historic marae (holy locations) that provide insight into customs and rituals from the past. Attend exciting cultural events that feature Tahitian music and dance to experience the islands' vivacious rhythms and beautiful gestures.

4. Outdoor Activities: Adventurers can choose from a variety of outdoor activities in Tahiti. Divers and snorkelers can explore beautiful coral reefs and see a wide variety of aquatic life. Hiking paths take you through luxuriant forests and to breathtaking vistas. Tahiti's waters are perfect for water sports like boating, paddleboarding, and surfing.

5. Delights of the palate: French, Polynesian, and foreign influences are blended into the cuisine of Tahiti. Enjoy fresh seafood specialties like poisson cru (raw fish prepared in the way of the Tahitian Islands and marinated in coconut milk), together with tropical fruits like papaya and pineapple. Don't pass up the chance to sample Tahiti's well-known "roulottes," portable food trucks that provide a range of regional cuisine.

6. Luxury and Relaxation: Tahiti has a variety of opulent resorts and lodgings that offer a tranquil and opulent experience. Overwater bungalows are available at many facilities, giving visitors access to the island's azure lagoon and its unspoiled beauty.

7. Island-hopping: Tahiti is a jumping-off point for other alluring French Polynesian islands. You may easily travel from Tahiti to neighboring islands including Moorea, Huahine, Raiatea, and

Taha'a, each of which has its own distinct charms and attractions.

The mix of Tahiti's breathtaking scenery, colorful culture, and friendly people makes for an amazing vacation experience. Tahiti promises to enthrall your senses and leave you with priceless memories, regardless of whether you desire adventure, leisure, cultural immersion, or a combination of all three.

Exploring the capital city of Papeete

Tahiti Island is home to Papeete, the energetic capital of French Polynesia. Papeete offers a distinctive and thrilling urban experience with its bustling markets, lively waterfront, and a blend of French and Polynesian traditions. A sample of things you can discover in Papeete is shown below:

1. Le Marché: Visit Papeete's bustling market, Le Marché, to begin your exploration. Tropical fruits, vibrant flowers, regional crafts, and classic Polynesian goods are all available here. Browse the stalls while interacting with the friendly vendors and soaking up the lively ambiance.

2. Papeete Market: The Papeete Market is located right next to Le Marché. This covered market, which sells a wide range of fresh vegetables, regional handicrafts, apparel, and souvenirs, is a hive of activity. Try exotic fruits, local specialties like poisson cru (marinated raw fish), and take in the market's vivacious vitality.

3. Place Vai'ete: Visit this waterfront promenade in the evenings to eat at one of the "roulottes," or food carts. This is a well-liked gathering place for locals and tourists alike, offering a wide selection of tasty dining options, from local specialties to cuisines from around the world. Take advantage of the lively ambiance, delight

in mouthwatering cuisine, and possibly attend some live musical acts.

4. Papeete Harbor Front: Take a stroll along this picturesque promenade for breathtaking views of the harbor, the distant island of Moorea, and the busy port. Take in the refreshing ocean breeze, watch the boats and ships come and go, and unwind at waterfront cafes and restaurants.

5. Black Pearl Museum: Visit the Black Pearl Museum to learn more about the intriguing world of Tahitian black pearls. Discover how pearls are grown, view beautiful pearl jewelry, and understand the cultural and economic importance of these priceless gems to French Polynesia.

Visit the Cathedral of Notre-Dame de Papeete, a notable landmark in the city, for more information. The stunning stained glass windows of this stunning church, which has French architectural elements. To feel Papeete's spiritual side, take a moment of solitude or go to church.

7. Museum of Tahiti and the Islands: The Museum of Tahiti and the Islands is a great place to go if you want to learn more about the history and culture of French Polynesia. Explore its exhibits to learn more about the natural history, traditional crafts, navigational methods, and effects of European interaction in the area.

A lovely blend of urban charm, native culture, and exciting adventures can be found in Papeete. By touring the city, you can immerse yourself in the vibrant atmosphere and learn about the distinctive fusion of French and Polynesian influences. It also acts as a gateway to the remainder of Tahiti and French Polynesia.

contrasting landscapes between Tahiti Nui and Tahiti Iti

Tahiti Nui

Its name, "Big Tahiti," refers to the largest part of the French Polynesian island of Tahiti. It comprises the island's western region and is renowned for its imposing mountains, verdant valleys, and energetic cities. Here are some of Tahiti Nui's main attributes and draws:

1. Mount Orohena: Mount Orohena is the tallest mountain in French Polynesia, rising to a height of 2,241 meters (7,352 feet). It dominates the island's terrain and provides breathtaking all-encompassing views of Tahiti Nui. Adventuresome hikers can attempt a strenuous climb to the peak, while others can take in the mountain's scenery from a variety of vantage points.

2. Faa'a International Airport: Faa'a International Airport is the major entry point to Tahiti Nui and

is situated in the capital city of Papeete. It serves as a center for internal and international flights linking Tahiti with other locations and warmly welcomes tourists from all over the world. For travelers, the airport offers necessary amenities and services.

3. Papeete: Tahiti Nui is home to the vibrant capital of French Polynesia, Papeete. It has a lively atmosphere, modern conveniences, and a fusion of Polynesian and French traditions. Discover the colorful markets where you may find regional goods, crafts, and souvenirs, such as Le Marché. Visit historical locations including the Black Pearl Museum and the Cathedral of Notre-Dame. Enjoy the busy nightlife, delicious waterfront cuisine, and energetic city.

4. coastline Promenade: The picturesque Papeete Harbor Front runs the length of the city's coastline. It provides stunning views of the bay, Moorea Island off in the distance, and the busy port. Enjoy a leisurely stroll, the calming

atmosphere of waterfront cafes, and the crisp ocean wind.

5. Marae Sites: Tahiti Nui is the location of a number of marae sites, which are old groups of stone temples. For the Polynesian people, these locations are of immense cultural and historical value. These archeological sites provide visitors the chance to explore them, discover local customs and rituals, and learn more about the island's rich history.

Tahiti Nui is recognized for its breathtaking natural beauty. The island boasts stunning scenery, gushing waterfalls, and verdant valleys. To find the inside of the island's hidden gems, go on a guided tour or go on a trekking excursion.

7. Tahiti Pearl Regatta: If you visit Tahiti Nui in May, there's a chance you'll get to see the Tahiti Pearl Regatta. During this yearly sailing competition, sailors from all over the world race their boats through the breathtaking waters around Tahiti, Moorea, and Raiatea.

Tahiti Nui offers a mesmerizing fusion of urban delights, cultural encounters, and natural wonders. Tahiti Nui invites you to immerse yourself in its beauty and embrace the essence of French Polynesia, whether you're hiking through verdant valleys, taking in panoramic views from mountain tops, or exploring the energetic streets of Papeete.

Tahiti Iti

French Polynesia's island of Tahiti, which translates to "Small Tahiti," is smaller and less developed than the rest of the island. In contrast to Tahiti Nui, it is located in the eastern portion of the island and offers a more untamed and rocky scenery. Here are some of Tahiti Iti's main attributes and draws:

Tahiti Iti is renowned for its pristine beaches, which are hidden away and undeveloped. Long lengths of white and black sand cover the coastline, which is bordered by turquoise waters. Away from the masses, these immaculate beaches offer the ideal backdrop for unwinding, swimming, snorkeling, and sunbathing. Teahupoo Beach, Papenoo Beach, and Taiarapu Beach are a few of the well-known beaches.

2. Raw Natural Beauty: Tahiti Iti is known for its natural landscape and untamable wilderness. A mesmerizing and beautiful landscape is created by dense forests, high cliffs, and secluded coves. With possibilities for trekking, discovering secret waterfalls, and taking in the island's varied flora and fauna, nature lovers will adore the island's unadulterated beauty.

3. Te Pari Cliffs: The Te Pari Cliffs, which are on the island's southern coast, are one of its most notable features. Awe-inspiring scenery is created by these beautiful cliffs, which rise sharply from the water. Viewpoints and boat tours are available for those who want to experience the cliffs' magnificence up close.

4. Small, traditional Polynesian villages: Tahiti Iti is home to these communities, which provide a genuine look into the way of life there. Visit communities like Tautira and Teahupoo to meet the welcoming residents, discover their traditions, and see native crafts and practices in action. It is an opportunity to fully immerse oneself in Tahiti's rich cultural history.

5. Water Activities: For those who enjoy the water, Tahiti Iti is a paradise. In particular, Teahupoo is well known for its world-class surfing. It is well-known for having strong, difficult waves that draw pro surfers from all over the world. Additionally, the clear seas provide chances for paddleboarding, snorkeling, and exploring the fascinating undersea world.

6. Faarumai Waterfalls: The stunning Faarumai Waterfalls are situated in the Faarumai Valley, on the northeastern shore of Tahiti Iti. There is a calm and revitalizing ambiance created by these falling waterfalls and the surrounding lush

vegetation. Enjoy the natural splendor of this peaceful location by hiking through the valley to the waterfalls.

Unlike Tahiti Nui, Tahiti Iti offers a more undiscovered experience. It is a paradise for nature lovers, adventurers, and people who want to experience French Polynesia's untainted beauty because of its unspoiled beaches, rocky scenery, traditional towns, and water activities.

Tahiti Beaches

The magnificent beaches on Tahiti, the largest island in French Polynesia, are well known. Here are a few of Tahiti's best beaches, which offer natural beauty, glistening waves, and chances for relaxation and water sports:

1. Matira Beach (Bora Bora): Although Matira Beach is actually on the adjacent island of Bora Bora, it is frequently mentioned in vacation

plans for Tahiti. One of the prettiest beaches in the world is this lovely expanse of white sand. It has serene surroundings, blue waters, and palm palms that are ideal for swimming, sunbathing, and snorkeling.

2. Temae Beach (Moorea): Temae Beach is a stunning location that can be found on the island of Moorea, not far from Tahiti. Its lengthy expanse of beautiful white sand and sparkling waters make it the perfect location for swimming, picnics, and beachcombing. The beach also provides expansive views of the mountains around and the island of Tahiti.

3. Papenoo Beach (Tahiti Iti): Papenoo Beach is a wild and undeveloped beauty that can be found on the eastern side of Tahiti. This beach is well-liked by beachcombers and surfers due to its dark sand, strong waves, and scenic backdrop. The area's natural beauty is enhanced by the surrounding lush greenery and the neighboring river.

4. La Plage de Maui (Tahiti Nui): La Plage de Maui is a stunning white sand beach on Tahiti Nui that offers a tranquil and private atmosphere. It's a great place for swimming because of the tranquil waters, and the atmosphere is cool thanks to the coconut trees' shade and the little breeze. It's the ideal location for relaxing and taking in the peace and quiet of the island.

5. Tiahura Beach (Moorea): Tiahura Beach, another gorgeous beach on Moorea, enchants tourists with its beautiful sand and crystal-clear blue waters. The beach is well-known for having an abundance of marine life, making it a well-liked location for diving and snorkeling. Discover the aquatic environment, go for a swim with some colorful fish, and unwind here.

6. Plage de Toaroto (Tahiti): Situated on Tahiti's western coast, Plage de Toaroto is a popular destination for both locals and tourists. The palm-lined shoreline gives a tranquil setting, while the quiet lagoon offers safe swimming

conditions. It's a convenient and fun beach for a day out because it has amenities including picnic spots, showers, and food sellers.

These are just a few of Tahiti's numerous breathtaking beaches. These beaches offer an exceptional experience in the enchanted paradise of French Polynesia, whether you're looking for relaxation, water sports, or simply the beauty of nature.

Trails for hiking and natural areas

Numerous hiking paths and natural preserves are available in Tahiti and the nearby islands, allowing tourists to discover French Polynesia's breathtaking vistas and varied ecosystems. Here are some noteworthy nature preserves and hiking paths to take into account:

1. Fautaua Valley: Fautaua Valley is a well-liked hiking location in Tahiti Nui that is renowned for its lush flora, gushing waterfalls, and picturesque views. The trail passes by numerous waterfalls, including the magnificent Fautaua Waterfall, as well as deep jungles, streams, and other fords. You'll be rewarded for your somewhat difficult hike with stunning natural splendor.

2. Three Coconut Trees Pass (Col des Trois Cocotiers): The island of Tahiti Nui is seen from afar from this hiking track. The trek begins close to Papeete and takes you through forests and across ridges before arriving at the Three Coconut Trees Pass, where you can take in expansive views of the surrounding coastline and mountains.

3. Opunohu Valley: Opunohu Valley, a scenic nature reserve with a number of hiking paths, is situated on the island of Moorea. Take a stroll through the verdant valley, through pineapple farms, and climb to viewpoints for breathtaking views of the mountains and the bay. The ancient

marae (stone temple) at Fare Hape is one of the archaeological sites in the valley.

4. Belvedere Lookout: The Belvedere Lookout, which is located on the island of Moorea, provides breath-taking views over Opunohu Bay and Cook's Bay. The overlook offers a panoramic view of the verdant valleys, craggy peaks, and the gorgeous blue seas of the bays below and may be accessed by short hike or by car.

5. Te Pari Cliffs: Situated on Tahiti Iti's southern coast, the Te Pari Cliffs not only offer breathtaking vistas, but also present trekking options. You can enjoy magnificent views of the ocean and the untamed coastline as you hike along the cliffs. The difficult terrain gives the walk an exciting element.

6. Vaipahi Gardens: A botanical garden and natural reserve, Vaipahi Gardens is located on Tahiti's southern shore. The well-kept trails take you through lush tropical vegetation and display

a wide range of local flora and flowers. Enjoy the quiet atmosphere of this serene oasis by taking a leisurely stroll.

7. Tetiaroa Atoll: This private island and nature reserve, which is situated northwest of Tahiti, is renowned for its pristine beaches, abundant marine life, and varied bird populations. Visitors can learn about conservation initiatives, experience the island's ecosystems, and take guided excursions to appreciate the natural splendor of this protected refuge.

In French Polynesia, it's crucial to be equipped with the right footwear, sun protection, insect repellant, and lots of water before starting any trekking excursion. Check local laws and get advice from tourism offices or knowledgeable guides on which trails might need a guide or permits. These nature preserves and hiking routes provide you the chance to fully experience French Polynesia's natural splendor and make lifelong memories of its breathtaking vistas.

Cultural Events and Holidays

There are numerous cultural events and festivals that provide tourists a deeper understanding of the local traditions and customs in French Polynesia, which includes Tahiti and Bora Bora. The following list of prominent local festivals and cultural events includes:

1. Heiva: During the month of July, Tahiti hosts the bright and extensively observed Heiva event. Locals display their traditional dances, music, crafts, and sports during this important cultural event. Visitors can take in enthralling performances, such as the well-known Tahitian dance "Ori Tahiti," as well as customary sporting events like canoe races and stone hoisting.

2. Marae Visits: Maraes are historic and culturally significant ancient sacred locations in

Polynesian culture. These complexes of stone temples served as the focal points of social and religious life in the past. Maraes offer visitors the chance to explore them and learn about their spiritual significance, customs, and island history. Marae Taputapuatea, which is located on the island of Raiatea and is regarded as the most important marae in French Polynesia, is one such marae.

French Polynesia is recognized for its excellent art and workmanship. 3. Polynesian Art & Crafts. Intricate woodcarvings, woven baskets, traditional costumes, and colorful pareos (sarongs) are just a few examples of the handcrafted goods shown by local craftsmen in markets like Le Marché in Papeete, which tourists can explore. These markets offer a great chance to support regional craftspeople and buy one-of-a-kind mementos.

4. Polynesian cuisine: Food plays a big part in any culture, so getting a taste of the native fare is a must if you want to really experience Tahiti

and Bora Bora culture. Try traditional Polynesian foods including taro, fei (a type of banana), poisson cru (raw fish marinated in coconut milk), and other tropical fruits. Numerous resorts and eateries offer Polynesian-themed dinners and cultural events where you may take in a delectable feast while taking in traditional music and dance displays.

5. Traditional Polynesian tattoos: The practice of getting a tattoo in this region has significant cultural and historical importance. Tatau, or Tahitian tattoos, are elaborate designs that both convey stories and signify ancestry. Visitors can choose to obtain a traditional tattoo from talented local tattoo artists and learn about the tattooing process and its symbolism.

6. Pearl farms: The glossy black pearls of French Polynesia are world-famous. Visitors can go on tours of pearl farms where they can discover more about the process of pearl farming, see demonstrations of pearl harvesting, and even buy fine pearl jewelry as a souvenir of their trip.

7. Traditional dance and music performances: Cultural centers and resorts all throughout Tahiti and Bora Bora offer enthralling dance and music performances. These performances feature traditional Polynesian dances backed by chants and drumbeats. It's a wonderful chance to take in the graceful elegance of Tahitian dance and the hypnotic rhythms of Polynesian music.

Visitors are able to admire the art, traditions, and history of the islands by participating in these cultural activities and festivals, which offer a look into the diverse past of French Polynesia. They provide a special and engaging method to engage with the community and make enduring memories of your trip to Tahiti and Bora Bora.

The Pearl of the Pacific "Bora Bora".

The French Polynesian island of Bora Bora, also known as the "Pearl of the Pacific," is a tropical haven. Bora Bora is a place that catches the imagination and leaves tourists in wonder. It is famous for its unique blue lagoon, immaculate white-sand beaches, and spectacular views. Here is a description of this beautiful island:

1. Unmatched Natural Beauty: Bora Bora is known for its extraordinary natural beauty. The island is encircled by a captivating lagoon, shielded by a barrier reef, which creates a tranquil, turquoise paradise with crystal-clear waters. The island's lush, volcanic Mount Otemanu and Mount Pahia rise sharply from its center, adding to its natural beauty.

2. Overwater Bungalows: Overwater bungalows are an iconic feature of Bora Bora and provide a distinctive and opulent lodging option. Guests

who stay in these lovely bungalows can awaken to expansive views of the lagoon, direct access to the clear waters, and the height of tropical luxury.

3. Snorkeling and Diving: The lagoon of Bora Bora is a sanctuary for snorkelers and divers because of the abundance of marine life there. Unforgettable underwater adventures are provided by the vibrant coral gardens, an abundance of tropical species, and even encounters with calm manta rays and reef sharks. The vivid underwater life may be explored in an ideal setting thanks to the warm waters and great visibility.

4. Matira Beach: Matira Beach is among the most beautiful stretches of sand in Bora Bora. Due to its fine white sand and clean waters, it is a well-liked location for swimming, sunbathing, and leisurely strolls. Matira Beach is the definition of a tropical paradise with its waving palm trees and lovely surroundings.

5. Hike up Mount Otemanu: Adventuresome tourists can set out on a difficult but worthwhile hike up Mount Otemanu. This volcanic mountain provides stunning 360-degree views of Bora Bora and the lagoon that surrounds it. Physical fitness is required for the hike, and knowledgeable guides are advised for safety.

6. Coral Gardens: The island of Bora Bora is home to a number of colorful coral gardens where snorkelers may see a rainbow of hues beneath the surface of the ocean. The marine life in these protected regions is abundant and includes coral reefs, tropical fish, and even stingray sightings. A must-do activity is to go on a guided snorkeling cruise to see the coral gardens.

7. Sunset cruises: Bora Bora is known for its mesmerizing sunsets. Many tour companies provide sunset cruises where you may unwind on a boat, drink tropical drinks, and observe as the sky over the lagoon changes into a pallet of

brilliant colors. It's a memorable and romantic experience.

Bora Bora is an ideal location for honeymooners, nature lovers, and those wanting a genuine tropical retreat because of its breathtaking natural scenery, opulent lodgings, and plentiful marine life. The island of Bora Bora promises a memorable experience that truly lives up to its nickname as the "Pearl of the Pacific," whether you decide to unwind on the beach, scuba dive, or simply take in the natural beauty of the island.

Overview of Bora Bora

Welcome to Bora Bora, a real tropical paradise and the crowning achievement of French Polynesia. The South Pacific island of Bora Bora is well-known across the world for its magnificent beauty, pristine waters, and picturesque scenery. For tourists looking for a piece of paradise, Bora Bora provides an amazing experience with its famed overwater bungalows, bright coral reefs, and beautiful volcanic peaks.

You will be enchanted by this island's picture-perfect landscape as soon as you arrive. As far as the eye can see, a turquoise lagoon is enclosed by a colorful coral reef, providing a calm haven for marine life and water sports aficionados. The island's central mountain ranges, Mount Otemanu and Mount Pahia, soar magnificently into the sky, adding a stunning background to the already attractive surroundings.

Luxury resorts and stunning overwater bungalows are two of Bora Bora's most well-known features. With panoramic views and easy access to the lagoon's tempting turquoise waters, these opulent rooms let visitors fully enjoy the grandeur of the setting. Imagine walking off the terrace of your private cottage and into a balmy lagoon dotted with bright coral gardens and tropical fish.

Every kind of traveler can find something to do on the island. Divers and snorkelers can scuba dive and explore the coral gardens, swim with rays, and take in the diverse marine life. Hiking trails can be taken by adventurers to stunning viewpoints with expansive views of the island and lagoon. The gorgeous beaches, such Matira Beach, offer a tranquil backdrop for visitors wishing to unwind, soak up the sun, or partake in water sports like paddleboarding and kayaking.

You'll come across friendly natives who take pleasure in their heritage as you immerse yourself in Bora Bora's unique culture. You will have the chance to see spectacular dance performances, savor authentic Polynesian food, and discover the island's interesting history. The rich Polynesian traditions and customs are woven into the fabric of daily life.

Bora Bora offers an unmatched experience that will astound you, whether you're celebrating a special occasion, looking for a romantic holiday, or simply wishing for an escape to paradise. Bora Bora is a place that will beyond your wildest expectations and make memories that will last a lifetime, from its immaculate beaches and opulent lodgings to its teeming marine life and magnificent surroundings. Welcome to this paradise in the tropics, where leisure and beauty have no boundaries.

The Famous Overwater Villas

The recognizable overwater bungalows that dot the blue lagoon are one of the first pictures that spring to mind when thinking of Bora Bora. These distinctive lodgings, which have come to represent luxury, provide visitors to the island a remarkable experience. Here is a closer look at Bora Bora's famous overwater bungalows:

1. Unparalleled Location: Strategically constructed on stilts above the serene lagoon,

Bora Bora's overwater bungalows provide unrivaled access to the region's pure seas and breath-taking vistas. Step outside onto your private terrace to take in the vibrant marine life swimming beneath you or to simply take in the tranquility of the lagoon and the surrounding splendor of nature.

2. Luxurious Amenities: These bungalows are made to be as comfortable and luxurious as possible. They have roomy interiors with contemporary furnishings, comfortable beds, and well-equipped bathrooms. For a truly opulent experience, several bungalows also feature outdoor bathrooms, Jacuzzis, and private plunge pools.

3. Direct Lagoon Access: Direct access to the lagoon is one of the key benefits of booking an overwater house. Most bungalows include a private ladder or staircase that descends into the invitingly warm ocean. From your front door, you may swim, snorkel, or kayak to fully experience Bora Bora's natural splendor.

4. Panoramic Views: The lagoon and the surroundings may be seen in all their splendor from the overwater bungalows. From your room, you can take in breath-taking sunrises and sunsets, the vivid hues of the lagoon, and the tranquil atmosphere of the water spreading out in front of you. Some bungalows have glass floors and big windows so you may enjoy the aquatic environment without leaving your accommodation.

5. Privacy and Seclusion: The overwater bungalows in Bora Bora offer an unparalleled sense of privacy and seclusion. In order to provide maximum solitude, several resorts have placed the bungalows carefully. This enables visitors to enjoy their own personal paradise. The peace and quiet provided by these upscale lodgings are enjoyable whether you're relaxing on your deck or swimming in the lagoon.

6. Romantic atmosphere: Bora Bora's overwater bungalows have come to be associated with

romance. These lodgings have a seductive appeal for newlyweds looking for a private retreat as well as for couples looking for a romantic holiday. The exquisite location, combined with the opulent amenities and tranquility, creates the ideal environment for romance and special occasions.

An experience that blends luxury, unmatched natural beauty, and the distinct character of French Polynesia is staying in an overwater house in Bora Bora. It's an opportunity to experience the mesmerizing surroundings, indulge in first-rate hospitality, and make priceless memories in one of the most stunning locations on Earth.

The pristine beaches of Bora Bora

The pristine beaches at Bora Bora are among the most breathtaking in the world. Visitors to the island can enjoy a piece of paradise at these beaches, which include fine white sand, blue waters, and a calm atmosphere. Here are a few of Bora Bora's best beaches:

1. Matira Beach: Matira Beach is frequently considered as one of the South Pacific's most beautiful beaches. It is a lengthy stretch of fine white sand that gently slopes into the lagoon and is found on the southernmost point of the main island. The area's tranquil waters are excellent for swimming and snorkeling. Palm trees flank the beach, offering shady areas to unwind and take in the spectacular views.

2. One Foot Island: This tiny islet, which is part of the Bora Bora archipelago, is well-known for its pristine beaches and unspoiled natural beauty. The term "One Foot Island" refers to a well-known photo opportunity where tourists can stand in the water with one foot on a signpost that marks the southernmost point of the Cook Islands. Fine white sand, clean waters,

and a serene ambience make this beach feel like a true tropical getaway.

3. Matira Point: With its sandy shoreline and calm waters, Matira Point, which is close to Matira Beach, offers a gorgeous environment. The beach is a fantastic location for picnicking, sunbathing, and leisurely stroll along the shore. Be sure to stay until the evening to see Matira Point's breathtaking sunsets, which are equally well-known for them.

4. Coral Garden: Although it's not a typical sandy beach, Bora Bora's Coral Garden is a must-see location for snorkeling fans. The Coral Garden, next to the barrier reef, is a haven for a variety of vibrant coral formations and marine life. Put your snorkeling equipment on and explore this underwater paradise, where you'll see rays, tropical fish, and other intriguing aquatic life.

5. Sofitel Private Island: Situated on a secluded islet, the Sofitel Private Island is a five-star

hotel. A private beach with a sense of exclusivity can be found here. It's the ideal location for rest and renewal because to its immaculate sands and clean seas.

6. Motu Tapu: This tiny, uninhabited islet is a perfect example of Bora Bora's beauty. Motu Tapu is frequently depicted in postcards and travel guides because of its pure white sand and turquoise waters. Even though there are few opportunities to visit the islet, certain hotels provide day tours and excursions that let guests take in its unspoiled beauty.

You will be surrounded by the beauty and serenity that these unspoiled coasts have to offer, whether you prefer to unwind on Matira Beach, discover the underwater wonders of the Coral Garden, or locate your own private area. The beaches of Bora Bora are a true monument to French Polynesia's natural beauty and will leave you with priceless memories of your trip to a tropical paradise.

Snorkeling and diving in the Lagoons of Bora Bora

Discovering the colourful underwater world that exists beneath the surface is made possible by snorkeling and scuba diving in the lagoons of Bora Bora, which are incomparable experiences. Bora Bora offers some of the best snorkeling and diving possibilities in the world because to its blue waters, abundant marine life, and vibrant coral gardens. What you need to know is as follows:

1. Coral Gardens: The Coral Gardens in Bora Bora are a must-visit snorkeling location. These protected areas, which are found within the lagoon, are teaming with different coral forms, including gorgeous hard and soft corals. As you swim among tropical fish like parrotfish, butterflyfish, and angelfish, you'll see a kaleidoscope of hues. Watch out for rays and even small reef sharks, among other aquatic animals.

2. Anau Reef: Another well-liked snorkeling location, Anau Reef gives visitors the chance to explore a healthy coral habitat. This region, which is on the lagoon's outer edge, is well-known for its colorful coral walls and the profusion of marine life that resides there. Diverse fish species, such as triggerfish, surgeonfish, and wrasses, as well as the occasional sea turtle, can be seen by snorkelers.

3. Muri Muri: A remote region with tranquil waters and stunning coral formations, Muri Muri is located on the southeast side of Bora Bora. There are numerous tropical fish and vibrant coral gardens in this lagoon. Snorkelers can take in the serene atmosphere as they explore the underwater wonders and come across a wide variety of marine animals.

1. Tapu Dive Site: Tapu is a well-known dive site that is situated just outside the barrier reef of the lagoon. This location provides an exhilarating diving experience with the chance

to explore underwater overhangs, caverns, and swim-throughs. Diverse marine life, including as reef sharks, manta rays, eagle rays, and schools of vibrant fish, can be found in the area's waters.

2. Teavanui Pass: A passage that links the lagoon to the wide ocean is known as Teavanui Pass. Strong currents that draw bigger marine animals provide a spectacular diving experience. Pelagic species including barracudas, tuna, and occasionally even hammerhead sharks can be seen by divers. Due to the difficult conditions, this site is suggested for experienced divers only.

3. White Valley: White Valley, a diving location famed for its gorgeous coral gardens and clear seas, is situated on the northern side of Bora Bora. Divers may check out various coral formations, swim with schools of fish, and see fascinating underwater life like octopuses and moray eels.

It's critical to observe safety precautions, dive with recognized guides, and respect Bora Bora's delicate marine habitat before starting any snorkeling or diving trip. The lagoons of Bora Bora offer an immersive experience that will leave you in wonder of the colourful underwater world and leave you with lifelong memories of your trip to this tropical paradise, whether you're a licensed diver or a snorkeling enthusiast.

Mount Pahia and Mount Otemanu

Two recognizable volcanic peaks that dominate the scenery of Bora Bora are Mount Otemanu and Mount Pahia. A unique journey and the chance to see spectacular views of the island and its surrounding lagoon are provided by exploring these gorgeous mountains. What you should know about these breathtaking peaks is as follows:

1. Mount Otemanu: - Height and Shape: Mount Otemanu is the highest point in Bora Bora,

rising roughly 727 meters (2,385 feet) above sea level. It is a stunning volcanic remnant distinguished by its angular beauty and high peaks.

- Hiking to the Summit: Climbing Mount Otemanu's summit is a difficult and hard task that calls for planning and experience. The ascent is difficult, and some stretches can necessitate the use of climbing gear and expertise. It is advised to go on this hike with an expert guide.

- Panoramic Views: The breath-taking panoramic panorama that awaits climbers of Mount Otemanu is their reward. On a clear day, the entire island of Bora Bora, the glistening lagoon, the neighboring motus (little islets), and the enormous Pacific Ocean are all in view. The scene is incredibly breathtaking and a monument to the area's natural beauties.

2. Mount Pahia: - Height and Features: Mount Pahia, which rises to a height of roughly 661 meters (2,169 feet), is the second-highest mountain in Bora Bora. It is renowned for its

conical shape and green, densely vegetated slopes.

- Hiking and Climbing: Just like Mount Otemanu, Mount Pahia requires both physical fitness and a sense of adventure to hike and climb. The ascent is difficult and requires negotiating thorny bushes and steep elevation. It is best to go on this adventure with an experienced guide who can look out for your safety and provide local information.

Although Mount Pahia's peak may not be as reachable as Mount Otemanu, the hike through the lower slopes still gives breathtaking vistas and opportunities to fully appreciate Bora Bora's natural splendor. Exotic plants, gushing waterfalls, and glimmers of the island's varied ecosystem can all be seen as you climb.

It's vital to remember that these mountains should only be hiked or climbed by skilled local guides or by experienced hikers. Prioritizing safety while ascending is crucial because the terrain might be difficult. Even if you don't get it to the summits, exploring Mount Otemanu and

Mount Pahia's lower slopes still lets you take in their distinct beauty and majesty.

Mount Otemanu and Mount Pahia offer a fantastic connection to the natural beauties of Bora Bora, whether you prefer to take in their majesty from afar or set out on a strenuous hike. These majestic landmarks add to the island's attraction and offer once-in-a-lifetime opportunity to marvel at the untamed beauty and majesty of volcanic landscapes.

Luxury Resorts and Spas in Bora Bora

Bora Bora is well known for its opulent resorts and top-notch spas, which provide tourists with a taste of paradise and unrivaled indulgence. Here's a look at the island's luxurious lodgings and relaxing spa treatments:

1. Overwater Bungalows: Overwater bungalows in Bora Bora are renowned for being the height of luxury. These luxurious, private apartments are set over a lagoon and provide easy access to

the clear waters as well as breath-taking vistas. Each villa offers a luxury and private stay thanks to its tasteful design, modern conveniences, plush furnishings, and private decks or plunge pools.

2. Five-Star Resorts: Bora Bora is home to a selection of opulent resorts that serve affluent tourists. These resorts offer an exceptional vacation by fusing spectacular natural scenery, superb service, and exquisite architecture. Each resort, from well-known multinational chains to secluded boutique lodges, offers a special fusion of solitude, comfort, and luxury, ensuring a truly opulent experience.

3. Spa retreats: Bora Bora is known for its luxurious spas, which are known for their serene locations, knowledgeable therapists, and comprehensive treatment menus. Many hotels and resorts have their own on-site spas that provide a variety of luxurious services and wellness rituals. Enjoy relaxing treatments like massages, body wraps, facials, and other

revitalizing therapies that use natural ingredients and age-old methods to leave you feeling renewed.

4. Private Villas and Pools: Bora Bora's finest resorts frequently provide private villas and pools for customers wanting the utmost seclusion and exclusivity. These remote lodgings offer a calm escape where you can relax in your very own haven. Enjoy a romantic meal under the stars, relax in the Jacuzzi in your private infinity pool, and be surrounded by the unspoiled beauty of the island.

5. Fine dining: The luxury resorts in Bora Bora are renowned for their outstanding gastronomic offerings. Enjoy top-notch cuisine cooked by renowned chefs using a combination of foreign and Polynesian tastes. The gourmet cuisine in Bora Bora will definitely tempt your taste buds, whether you're eating on the beach, in an overwater restaurant, or in the privacy of your villa.

6. Water Sports and Activities: Bora Bora's resorts provide a variety of water sports and activities in addition to opulent lodging and spa services. There are several chances for adventure and exploration, from paddleboarding, kayaking, and jet skiing to snorkeling and diving in the colorful lagoon.

pleasure is personified in the opulent resorts and spas of Bora Bora, which offer a sanctuary of luxury and pleasure amidst the island's breathtaking natural beauty. Bora Bora's opulent amenities will undoubtedly surpass your expectations and leave you with enduring memories of unadulterated joy, whether you're looking for a romantic holiday, a honeymoon location, or simply a retreat to indulge yourself.

Natural Wonders of Bora Bora and Tahiti

Visitors are enthralled by the variety of natural treasures that Tahiti and Bora Bora have to offer. Here are some of the natural treasures you can discover in Tahiti and Bora Bora, from lush landscapes to clear waters:

1. Lush Rainforests: Tahiti and Bora Bora are both covered with lush rainforests that highlight the natural beauty of the islands. Hike through the thick undergrowth to see towering trees, colorful tropical flowers, and a chorus of chattering birds. The rainforests provide an immersive experience in nature since they are home to a diverse range of wildlife, including rare plant species and native birds.

2. Waterfalls: Both Tahiti and Bora Bora are filled with beautiful waterfalls that tumble from

rocky cliffs into glistening pools. The Fautaua Waterfall in Tahiti, which plunges from a height of 985 feet (300 meters), and the Vaioro Falls in Bora Bora, which may be reached via a beautiful hike, are two prominent waterfalls. The opportunity to swim or simply take in their breathtaking splendor is offered by these natural wonders, which also offer a refreshing respite.

3. Pristine Lagoons: Tahiti and Bora Bora's surrounding lagoons are in and of themselves natural wonders. The contrast between the lush flora and white sand beaches and the blue waters is breathtaking. These lagoons support thriving coral reefs, an abundance of marine life, and fascinating underwater vistas. You may explore this healthy ecosystem by snorkeling or scuba diving in the lagoons, where you'll see a variety of vibrant fish, rays, turtles, and even sharks.

4. Magnificent barrier reefs that protect the islands and make tranquil lagoons can be seen in Tahiti and Bora Bora. These reefs provide chances for snorkeling, diving, and underwater

exploration and are filled with a variety of marine life. Your underwater explorations are set against the vivid coral formations, which range from small branching corals to enormous brain corals.

5. Mount Otemanu: Mount Otemanu is a natural marvel that dominates the skyline of Bora Bora. This craggy volcanic mountain is not only beautiful from a distance, but it also presents challenging trekking and climbing chances. You are rewarded with breath-taking panoramic views of the island, lagoon, and surrounding motus when you climb Mount Otemanu.

6. Motus: The lagoons surrounding Tahiti and Bora Bora are dotted with countless motus, which are little islets. These motus have picture-perfect scenery with their immaculate beaches, coconut palm forests, and blue waters. You may fully experience the untamed beauty and tranquility of the islands by exploring these motus via boat cruises, kayaking, or paddleboarding.

These natural treasures of Tahiti and Bora Bora are evidence of French Polynesia's remarkable beauty. You will be delighted by the breathtaking scenery and the alluring delights that are waiting for you at every turn, whether you're hiking through rainforests, swimming in lagoons, or admiring the beautiful Mount Otemanu.

Beautiful Mountain Sceneries

In addition to their magnificent beaches and azure waters, Tahiti and Bora Bora are recognized for their verdant mountainous terrain. These mountainous areas provide chances for exploration and adventure as well as a distinctive contrast to the coastal splendor. Here's a closer look at Tahiti and Bora Bora's verdant mountain ranges:

1. Tahiti Nui: - The Valleys: Tahiti Nui, which makes up the majority of Tahiti, is distinguished by its lush valleys that slash through the mountains. The valleys, including the Papenoo Valley and the Fautaua Valley, are covered with luxuriant foliage, tumbling waterfalls, and lovely rivers. You can immerse yourself in the beauty of nature by hiking through these valleys and finding secret gems along the way. Mount Orohena is the highest peak in French Polynesia, reaching an amazing height of 2,241 meters (7,352 ft). The mountain, which is frequently shrouded in mist and encircled by thick forests, is a mesmerizing sight. While ascending the lower slopes offers the chance to experience the mountain's majestic presence and take in breath-taking views of the island, reaching the peak needs advanced mountaineering skills.

2. Bora Bora: Mount Otemanu and Mount Pahia: Mount Otemanu and Mount Pahia, two recognizable volcanic summits, provide more than just expansive views. Tropical flora abounds in the lush greenery that envelops these

mountains, flourishing in the volcanic soil. The lower slopes are covered in breadfruit trees, coconut palms, and other natural flora, which makes for a beautiful scene.

- Hiking paths: Bora Bora has a number of hiking paths that let you experience the island's hilly landscape. Trekking through the slopes and valleys surrounding Mount Otemanu and Mount Pahia provides views of the island's natural beauty, which includes thriving plant life, rare bird species, and expansive panoramas of the lagoon and neighboring motus.

You may disconnect from the hustle and bustle of the shore in Tahiti and Bora Bora's beautiful mountain vistas, where you can experience nature in a new environment. These mountainous areas offer a serene escape and a chance to take in the tremendous diversity of French Polynesia's natural beauty, whether you decide to stroll through valleys, look for hidden waterfalls, or simply enjoy the gorgeous peaks from a distance.

Swimmable holes and waterfalls

Many beautiful waterfalls and swimming holes may be found on Tahiti and Bora Bora, offering guests peaceful and revitalizing experiences. These natural treasures provide an opportunity to unwind, get back in touch with nature, and take in the calming sounds of falling water. The following swimming holes and waterfalls can be found in Tahiti and Bora Bora:

Tahiti: 1. Fautaua Waterfall: This magnificent waterfall is situated in the Fautaua Valley not far from Papeete. The waterfall descends into a peaceful lake from a height of around 985 feet (300 meters). You can reach this gorgeous location after a stroll through the lush rainforest, where you may cool off in the water or just take in the scenery.

2. Vaipahi Gardens: Although not a typical waterfall, Tahiti's Vaipahi Gardens include a tranquil stream that meanders through a tropical garden. Visitors can relax in the cold water and take in the tranquillity of the surroundings at the garden's numerous little cascades and natural pools.

1. Vaioro Falls: Situated in the beautiful interior of Bora Bora, Vaioro Falls is a jewel just waiting to be found. You can reach these beautiful waterfalls, which drop into natural pools below, after a beautiful stroll through the woods. You are invited to have a relaxing dip in the clear waters or to unwind amidst the breathtaking natural splendor.

2. Matira Beach: This beach is well-known for its crystal-clear waters and white-sand beaches, but it also has a delightful swimming hole called the "Matira Natural Pool." This quiet pool is the ideal place for a leisurely swim or wading. It is formed by natural rock formations.

It's important to respect nature and adhere to any rules or limitations set forth when visiting these waterfalls and swimming holes. Make sure to keep these locations tidy and beautiful so that visitors in the future can enjoy them.

In Tahiti and Bora Bora, waterfalls and swimming holes offer a cool respite from the tropical heat as well as opportunities for introspective reflection and relaxation. Whether you're looking for adventure or a quiet vacation, these natural havens will leave you feeling refreshed and spellbound by French Polynesia's unspoiled beauty.

Marine life and coral reefs

For divers and snorkelers, Tahiti and Bora Bora are paradises because of their abundant marine life and well-known coral reefs. The underwater world is a kaleidoscope of colors and a rich tapestry of marine species, which may be seen when exploring it. Here is a sample of the marine life and coral reefs you can see in Tahiti and Bora Bora:

1. Coral reefs: Coral reefs, which are famous for their beauty and biological significance, are abundant in the lagoons that surround Tahiti and Bora Bora. The lagoon waters are calm and shallow because these reefs create a protective barrier around the islands. You can discover coral gardens filled with both hard and soft corals, including brain corals, staghorn corals, and colorful coral formations. The reefs are a dynamic environment that serve as a home to numerous fish, crustacean, and other marine animals.

2. Color Fish: Tahiti and Bora Bora's waters are home to a dizzying variety of fish species, which may be seen while snorkeling or scuba diving there. You'll be immersed in a world of colorful marine life, from small, brightly colored tropical fish like butterflyfish, angelfish, and clownfish to larger species like groupers and parrotfish.

Watch out for the Moorish idol, a stunning fish that is frequently spotted close to coral structures. The lagoons also provide possibilities to see rays gliding over the water in a lovely manner.

3. Turtles: Tahiti and Bora Bora are well-known for their sea turtle populations, which include the green and hawksbill varieties. While snorkeling or scuba diving close to the coral reefs, one can frequently come across these exquisite creatures. A truly captivating experience is watching them float through the water with ease or seeing them surface for breath.

4. Sharks and rays: Several different species of sharks and rays call the lagoons of Tahiti and Bora Bora home. In particular in locations where they are protected, blacktip reef sharks and lemon sharks are frequently sighted. Stingrays, such as the elegant manta ray, can also be seen, providing a chance for up-close encounters and amazing adventures.

5. Additional Marine Life: Tahiti and Bora Bora's underwater environments are home to a staggering variety of marine life in addition to fish, turtles, sharks, and rays. Moray eels, octopuses, vibrant nudibranchs, and a range of crabs are among the marine life to look out for. If you're lucky, you might even see dolphins playing near your boat or catch a glimpse of whales migrating.

Responsible snorkeling and diving are crucial for the maintenance and preservation of these delicate ecosystems. Respect marine life by not touching or disturbing it, and abide by any rules and laws that may be in place locally.

The coral reefs and marine life of Tahiti and Bora Bora provide an enthralling insight into the wonders of the undersea world. You can appreciate the subtle beauty and delicate balance of nature by exploring these dynamic ecosystems, which will make your trip to French Polynesia an experience you won't soon forget.

Routes for Scenic Hiking and Trekking

There are several scenic hiking and trekking trails available in Tahiti and Bora Bora, which let you experience the natural beauty of the islands and discover their varied topographies. Here are some noteworthy routes to take into account, whether you enjoy mountain climbs, beach walks, or excursions through rain forests:

Tahiti:
1. Fautaua Valley: The Fautaua Valley, close to Papeete, is a well-liked trekking location. The trek leads to the magnificent Fautaua Waterfall after passing sparkling streams and beautiful woods. The hike combines stunning natural scenery with breathtaking vistas.

2. Three Waterfalls Hike: The Papenoo Valley, renowned for its breathtaking scenery, is the starting point of this trek. The Vaipoiri, Vaimahutu, and Putoa waterfalls are three

beautiful waterfalls that you pass while hiking through the valley. You'll pass by tropical flora, historic archeological sites, and breathtaking views along the way.

1. Mount Otemanu and Mount Pahia Hike: Climbing Mount Otemanu or Mount Pahia is an exhilarating experience for intrepid hikers. Both summits demand technical expertise and guidance, but the payoff is stunning panoramic views of the lagoon and neighboring motus on Bora Bora. These hikes offer a distinctive viewpoint of the island's breathtaking landscapes and are appropriate for experienced climbers.

2. Cross-Island Hike: You may explore Bora Bora's varied topography on this hike that takes you from one side of the island to the other. The walk offers breathtaking views of the lagoon and ocean as it winds through dense trees and up slopes. The hike offers a chance to take in the island's natural splendor while coming into contact with the indigenous flora and fauna.

It's crucial to be organized and take the appropriate safety precautions before starting any hiking or trekking adventure. Follow approved trails, carry enough water, and dress appropriately. It is advisable to speak with local tour operators or guides who can offer insightful advice, guarantee your safety, and improve your overall experience.

Discover hidden treasures, experience breath-taking vistas, and get in touch with nature on these beautiful hiking and trekking paths in Tahiti and Bora Bora. So prepare to explore the breathtaking landscapes of the islands on foot by packing your trekking supplies and donning some comfortable walking shoes.

Flora and fauna of the Islands

The islands of Tahiti and Bora Bora exhibit the distinct ecosystems and breathtaking beauty of French Polynesia through their diverse flora and fauna. Here is a sample of the fascinating plants and animals you can find on these islands:

Flora: 1. Coconut palms, which are typical of tropical islands and adorn the coasts of Tahiti and Bora Bora, add to the beauty of the surroundings. The adaptable coconut tree offers food, shade, and supplies for a variety of traditional crafts.

2. Breadfruit Trees: The breadfruit tree, also called as "uru" in Tahitian, is another notable tree in the area. Large, imposing trees produce spherical, green fruits that, when cooked, have a texture like to bread. A mainstay of Polynesian cuisine, breadfruit has cultural significance in the customs of the region.

3. Tiare Flower: The tiare flower has a unique position in Tahitian culture and is the national flower of French Polynesia. Its delicate, white petals have a lovely scent and are frequently utilized as decorations in traditional dances and

celebrations or as embellishments for flower crowns.

4. Tropical Fruits: Papaya, pineapple, mango, passion fruit, guava, and other tropical fruits are widely available in Tahiti and Bora Bora. In addition to pleasing the palate, these luscious and tasty fruits also contribute to the lushness of the island sceneries.

Fish and marine life abound in the waters between Tahiti and Bora Bora, with a dizzying variety of marine species. Coral reefs are home to vibrant creatures including butterflyfish, angelfish, triggerfish, and clownfish. Turtles, rays (including manta rays and eagle rays), reef sharks, and other kinds of crabs are examples of additional marine life.

2. Birds: Several endemic bird species can be found in French Polynesia. Birds including the Tahiti kingfisher, Tahiti reed warbler, and the recognizable black paradise flycatcher inhabit the islands. These species, which contribute to

the avian richness of the islands, are frequently seen in their native environments.

3. Land Crabs: The coconut crab, which is the largest land-dwelling arthropod in the world, lives in Tahiti and Bora Bora. These amazing organisms can be seen in some places, especially in coastal settings, and they are quite important to ecosystems.

4. Whales and dolphins: Different whale species use the waters of Tahiti and Bora Bora as a migration path. Visitors may have the chance to see humpback whales, sperm whales, orcas, and other cetaceans during the whale-watching season. Spinner dolphins and bottlenose dolphins, two species of dolphins, are commonly spotted playing and leaping through the waves.

You can understand the distinctive biodiversity of Tahiti and Bora Bora by investigating its flora and wildlife. You will be enthralled by the natural beauty and the interconnection of the ecosystems that make up these paradisiacal locations, whether diving in brilliant coral gardens or exploring lush jungles.

Outdoor Adventures and Activities

For those looking for adventure and excitement, Tahiti and Bora Bora offer a wide range of outdoor pursuits. Here are some well-liked possibilities to think about, ranging from land excursions to water-based ones:

1. Snorkeling and diving: Tahiti and Bora Bora are havens for snorkelers and divers thanks to their vivid coral reefs and crystal-clear lagoons. Discover the undersea realm where you can see rays, turtles, fish of all colors, and other marine life. There are several diving and snorkeling areas, from beginner-friendly sites to more challenging locales for seasoned divers.

2. Jet skiing and other water activities: Jet skiing across the islands' surrounding seas will give you an adrenaline boost. To explore the lagoons, visit distant motus (islets), and experience the rush of speed on the water, rent a jet ski or embark on a guided tour. Other water sports that offer countless hours of fun and adventure include kayaking, paddleboarding, kiteboarding, and parasailing.

3. Bodyboarding and Surfing: Surfers from all over the world travel to Tahiti to experience its world-class surf breakers. Particularly known for its enormous, strong waves, Teahupo'o is sometimes regarded as one of the world's most difficult surf locations. Tahiti's surf breaks offer an exhilarating experience whether you're an expert surfer or a beginner looking to catch some smaller waves. Bodyboarding is also well-liked and offers a practical method of riding the waves.

4. 4x4 Safari Tours: Take a thrilling 4x4 safari tour to experience Tahiti and Bora Bora's

untamed landscapes. Explore the interior of the islands, moving through verdant valleys, through rivers, and up mountains for spectacular panoramic views. A unique and educational adventure will be provided by knowledgeable guides who will give insights into the ecology, fauna, and cultural history of the islands.

5. Hiking & Trekking: Pull on your boots and explore the picturesque paths of the islands. There are alternatives for all levels of fitness, from mountain excursions to rainforest hikes. Explore indigenous plant species, find secret waterfalls, and take in expansive views of the aquamarine lagoons. The Fautaua Valley in Tahiti and the climbs up Mount Otemanu and Mount Pahia in Bora Bora are well-known hiking destinations.

6. Ziplining: Feel the rush as you soar through the thick canopy of a forest. Both Tahiti and Bora Bora offer a variety of zipline courses that provide a distinctive viewpoint of the islands' natural surroundings. Fly through the trees while

experiencing an adrenaline rush and taking in the surrounding scenery.

7. Island Excursions & Boat Tours: Take a guided boat tour or a solo excursion to discover the nearby islands and motus. In the presence of knowledgeable experts, explore secret coves, remote beaches, and snorkeling locations. Discover the history and culture of the islands, take in the breathtaking coral gardens of the lagoons, and take in the archipelago's natural splendor.

By engaging in these outdoor pursuits and excursions in Tahiti and Bora Bora, you'll be able to appreciate the natural marvels of the islands, have exhilarating experiences, and make lifelong memories. French Polynesia has an experience waiting for every kind of adventurer, whether they like land excursions, water-based pursuits, or a combination of the two.

Water sports include diving, jet skiing, and snorkeling.

Due to its famed spectacular natural beauty and crystal-clear waters, Tahiti and Bora Bora are perfect locations for a variety of watersports. An overview of jet skiing, diving, and snorkeling in Tahiti and Bora Bora is provided below:

Snorkeling: Because of the rich marine life and bright coral reefs, snorkeling is a well-liked pastime in both Tahiti and Bora Bora. Numerous hotels and tour companies offer snorkeling excursions that transport you to the best snorkeling locations, like coral gardens and lagoons. These places offer fantastic chances to get up close and personal with colorful fish, coral formations, and other fascinating aquatic life. To explore the underwater environment at your leisure, you can either rent snorkeling equipment or bring your own.

Dive destinations Tahiti and Bora Bora provide excellent diving opportunities for both novice and expert divers. Sharks, rays, tropical fish, and coral gardens can all be found in the pure waters. Your safety while exploring the underwater treasures is guaranteed by the many dive centers and resorts that offer guided diving trips and dive training. You can explore underwater caverns, canyons, and drop-offs, each of which offers a distinctive diving experience.

Jet skiing is a thrilling water sport that lets you swiftly and with enthusiasm explore the beautiful shores of Tahiti and Bora Bora. Many resorts provide guided tours and jet ski rentals so you can explore the local islands and lagoons. Jet skiing enables you to explore the clear waters, take in the cooling sea breeze, and take in the breathtaking scenery from a different angle. But make sure you follow the rules and safety precautions that the rental companies have established.

It's important to keep in mind that water quality and accessibility to these activities may change depending on the location, the local climate, and the amenities provided by various resorts or tour companies. For the latest recent advice and recommendations on watersports in Tahiti and Bora Bora, it's a good idea to check with local businesses or your lodging.

Spots for Kiteboarding and Surfing

There are a few places in French Polynesia that provide excellent possibilities for these water sports, albeit Tahiti and Bora Bora aren't particularly well renowned for their surfing and kiteboarding areas. Here are a few prominent locations in the area:

1. Teahupoo, Tahiti: Teahupoo is well-known among surfers for its storied and potent reef break. It is renowned for producing some of the largest and most difficult waves in the entire planet. Surfers who are experienced and skilled converge on Teahupo'o to prove their prowess and ride its legendary barrels.

2. Papara, Tahiti: Papara, which lies on the island's southwest shore, has a more accessible surfing environment than Teahupo'o. It offers a range of breakers, including reef breaks and beach breaks, that are appropriate for different skill levels. Local surfers and others seeking a less strenuous surfing experience frequently favor Papara.

One of the most well-known locations for kiteboarding is Motu Martin, an islet off the coast of Bora Bora. It's a great place for kiteboarding enthusiasts due to its small lagoon and reliable trade winds. The experience is enhanced by the gorgeous surroundings and the crystal-clear waters.

2. Moorea: Moorea still has some kiteboarding chances, despite not being as well-known for it as Bora Bora. The island has a number of windy lagoons that offer kiteboarding enthusiasts a magnificent setting in which to practice their sport.

As waves and wind conditions might change throughout the year, it is advised to check with nearby kiteboarding or surf schools for the most recent information on the finest locations and ideal times to engage in these activities. Before attempting these sports in potentially hazardous conditions, it's also critical to have the requisite knowledge and expertise.

Experiences with Yachting and Sailing

Tahiti and Bora Bora are great locations for sailing and yachting because they provide a wealth of picturesque locations and tranquil waters to explore. You can enjoy the following sailing and yachting activities in the area:

1. Island hopping: Tahiti and Bora Bora are ideal for island hopping excursions due to their scenic scenery and gorgeous lagoons. To explore the neighboring islands, including Moorea, Raiatea,

Huahine, and Taha'a, you can hire a sailboat or charter a yacht. Sailing between the islands lets you take your time exploring each one's splendor at your own speed.

2. Sunset Cruises: Take a sunset cruise to see stunning sunsets over the Pacific Ocean. Many tour companies provide sailing or boat experiences that are especially intended to catch the magnificent moments as the sun sets. As the sky changes into a rainbow of colors, relax in the tranquility, sip on cool beverages, and admire the beauty of the nearby islands.

3. Snorkeling and diving excursions: Add undersea exploration to your sailing or yachting adventure. Numerous sailing and yacht charters provide snorkeling and diving tours to top locations where you can see the thriving marine life and breathtaking coral reefs. Immerse yourself in the beauty of the undersea world by diving into crystal-clear waters where you will find a variety of fish, rays, and even sharks.

4. Luxury Yacht Charters: A luxury yacht can be rented if you want a top-notch sailing experience. To assure your pleasure and happiness, these boats are outfitted with opulent facilities and a qualified crew. As you cruise over the calm seas, enjoying individualized services and dining in delicious meals made by aboard chefs, experience the height of luxury.

5. Regattas and Sailing Events: If you're an expert sailor or simply an admirer of sailing, think about taking part in or watching regattas and sailing events hosted in Tahiti and Bora Bora. These gatherings of sailors from all around the world provide exciting competitions and a chance to interact with other sailing aficionados.

Working with trustworthy charter firms or tour operators is advised when organizing a sailing or yachting experience. They may help with route planning, choosing the best boat, and making sure the trip is safe and fun.

Deep-Sea Excursions for Fishing

Fishing enthusiasts looking for exhilarating adventures and the potential to capture a variety of large game fish frequently go deep sea fishing in Tahiti and Bora Bora. What you should know about deep-sea fishing trips in the area is as follows:

1. Fishing Charters: In Tahiti and Bora Bora, there are numerous fishing charters and tour companies that provide deep-sea fishing experiences. Experienced captains and crew members who are familiar with the regional fishing sites and methods are offered by these excursions. They typically supply the tackle, bait, and gear required for fishing, making sure you have everything you need for a productive outing.

2. Fishing Spots: Tahiti and Bora Bora's surrounding waters provide fantastic prospects

for deep-sea fishing. Many different species of game fish are drawn to the deep canals, reefs, and drop-offs. Marlin, yellowfin tuna, mahi-mahi, wahoo, and sailfish are among the frequently caught species. Depending on the time of year and the species being fished, the fishing locations can change.

3. Methods: On deep-sea fishing trips, various methods of fishing may be used. A common technique is trolling, which involves dragging lines loaded with lures or bait behind the boat as it moves slowly. Targeting fish like marlin and tuna is effective with this method. Fish like snapper and grouper can also be caught by bottom fishing with weighted lines and bait.

4. Length and Route: Depending on your preferences and availability, deep-sea fishing expeditions can range from half-day outings to full-day adventures. The itineraries often involve cruising to the fishing locations, engaging in active fishing for a few hours, and then sailing back to where you were. Some charters may also

offer onboard refreshments, meals, or snacks to keep you fueled up while you're traveling.

5. Regulations and Conservation: It's critical to understand the local fishing laws and conservation measures. To save the ecology, some fishing techniques may be prohibited and certain species may be subject to size and catch restrictions. The sustainability of the sport can be preserved by using ethical fishing techniques, such as catch-and-release for specific species.

It is advised to reserve in advance and let the fishing charter or tour operator know your preferences when organizing a deep-sea fishing adventure. They can inform you of the ideal times of year to catch a particular type of fish, the ideal length of your trip, and any other services or amenities that might be offered.

Exploring grottoes and caves

Exploring caves and grottoes can be a thrilling and adventurous pastime that provides a special chance to see nature's undiscovered beauties. There are a few significant places in the area where you can go cave exploring, even though Tahiti and Bora Bora may not have a lot of natural caves and grottoes:

1. Maraa Grotto, Tahiti: Maraa Grotto is a well-known location for cave exploration and is situated in the Papenoo Valley on the island's east coast. The grotto has a tranquil environment, a beautiful stalactite formation, and an underground river. To ensure a secure and educational experience, you can join guided tours or employ regional experts.

2. Ana Aotearoa, Raiatea: Ana Aotearoa is a magnificent cave system located on Raiatea, a neighboring island to Tahiti. The ancient rock art

and ethereal ambience of Ana Aotearoa add to the site's cultural value. The assistance of skilled guides who can share details about the history and tales of the caverns is necessary when exploring them.

3. Fa'anui Caves, Bora Bora: The Fa'anui Caves are a hidden gem in Bora Bora, which is more known for its gorgeous lagoons and overwater villas. These limestone caverns provide a distinctive underground environment. You can travel with local guides who can inform you about the cave's geological characteristics and the legends surrounding it.

Prioritizing safety is crucial when exploring grottoes and caverns. These are some general pointers:

- Always travel with seasoned guides who are familiar with the caverns and can guarantee your safety.

- Put on appropriate clothing and footwear that can handle potentially muddy and damp circumstances.

- Carry a dependable light source, such a headlamp or flashlight, to get around in the caves' pitch-black interior.

- To minimize hazards, adhere to the directions and recommendations supplied by the guides.

- Be mindful of your surroundings and refrain from touching or destroying any cave structures.

It should be noted that there may be less opportunities for cave exploring in Tahiti and Bora Bora than there are for other activities in the area, so it is best to check with local tour companies or visitor centers for the most recent information.

Exploring Nearby Islands

Discovering the distinct beauty of the area and extending your Tahiti and Bora Bora trip is made possible by seeing the adjacent islands. Here are a few nearby islands that are worth visiting:

1. Moorea: Moorea is regarded as Tahiti's "sister island" and is only a short ferry or boat trip away. It offers stunning natural scenery, including verdant mountains, aquamarine lagoons, and immaculate beaches. You can go hiking, snorkeling, or you can just unwind and take in the island's natural beauty. The Moorea Dolphin Center is located on Moorea, where you can experience a magical dolphin encounter.

2. Raiatea: The second-largest island in French Polynesia and frequently referred to as the

"Sacred Island," Raiatea is renowned for its extensive cultural and historical significance. Discover historic marae (classic Polynesian temples), verdant valleys, and breathtaking waterfalls. The gorgeous island of Taha'a, well-known for its vanilla plantations and natural beauty, may also be reached from Raiatea.

3. Huahine: Huahine is a serene, less-populated island that gives visitors a look at traditional Polynesian culture. It is renowned for its historical attractions, verdant scenery, and immaculate beaches. Learn about the island's past and become a part of the community by visiting the Fare Pote'e cultural center.

4. Tetiaroa: This private atoll, which lies a little farther away from Tahiti, was originally Marlon Brando's special getaway. The atoll is home to undeveloped white sand beaches, pristine waters, and a variety of marine life. Go snorkeling or diving, explore the island's natural splendor, and

discover the conservation initiatives being used to preserve this unique ecosystem.

5. Maupiti: Maupiti is a hidden gem if you're seeking for a location that is somewhat off the beaten path. This tiny island provides a serene and traditional Polynesian experience. Enjoy the gorgeous beaches, unspoiled environment, and coral gardens. You can see the entire lagoon by climbing Mount Teurafaatiu, the highest point on the island.

Take into account the various modes of transportation, including domestic flights, private boat charters, and ferry services, while organizing your island excursion. Make the most of your time and interests by researching and making travel plans for each island's distinct charms and activities.

A Tropical Paradise: Moorea

In fact, Moorea is a tropical paradise and a top choice for tourists looking for unspoiled scenery and a laid-back island lifestyle. Here are some details on what makes Moorea such an alluring tropical destination:

Moorea is renowned for its stunning scenery, which feature imposing mountain peaks, verdant valleys, and pristine lagoons. The island's skyline is dominated by the recognizable Mount Rotui and Mount Mouaroa, which serve as a lovely backdrop. Hiking through verdant paths, taking picturesque drives, or just taking in the view from your resort are all excellent ways to discover the island's natural splendor.

2. Beautiful Beaches: Moorea is home to gorgeous white-sand beaches that are palm-fringed and offer a paradise-like setting for sunbathing, swimming, and beach activities. Popular beaches include Les Tipaniers, a public

beach that is great for picnics and snorkeling, and Temae Beach, which is well-known for its tranquil waters and stunning views of Tahiti.

3. Abundant Marine Life: Moorea is surrounded by waters that are alive with marine life, making it a refuge for divers and snorkelers. A great variety of tropical fish, rays, and even sharks can be found in the coral gardens. To discover the underwater delights, including the well-known snorkeling location known as the Lagoonarium, snorkeling or diving tours can be planned.

4. Adventure Activities: Moorea has a ton of thrilling adventure activities to choose from. You can take an ATV excursion to see the island's untamed interior or go trekking in the verdant valleys or zip-lining among the treetops. Other well-liked ways to enjoy the lagoon include kayaking, paddleboarding, and jet skiing.

5. Cultural Experiences: Participate in traditional activities and visit cultural sites in Moorea to fully immerse yourself in Polynesian culture. A

polynesian dance performance, traditional arts like painting or weaving pareo (sarongs), or a trip to the Tiki Village to learn about the culture's history, music, and dance are all options.

6. Moorea is renowned for its unique overwater bungalows, which provide an opulent and romantic experience. When you stay in one of these bungalows, you may have immediate access to the ocean for swimming and snorkeling as well as breathtaking views of the lagoon when you wake up.

Moorea's tropical beauty and variety of activities make it a wonderfully alluring destination, whether you're looking for relaxation, adventure, or a romantic getaway. Moorea offers a tropical paradise experience that is difficult to resist with its picture-perfect landscape and warm Polynesian hospitality.

The Sacred Islands are Raiatea and Taha'a.

The "Sacred Islands," also known as Raiatea and Taha'a, are two adjacent islands in French Polynesia that provide a special fusion of scenic beauty, rich cultural history, and a serene ambiance. What makes Raiatea and Taha'a unique is as follows:

1. Raiatea has significant cultural and historical significance in Polynesian history. It was originally the epicenter of ancient Polynesian civilisation and is regarded as the spiritual and cultural core of French Polynesia. Several marae (holy temples) and ancient sites can be found in Raiatea, including the well-known Marae Taputapuatea, which is a UNESCO World Heritage Site. Visitors can tour these historic locations and discover more about the prehistoric Polynesian practices and beliefs.

2. Vanilla Plantations: Taha'a is referred to as the "Vanilla Island" because to the large number of vanilla plantations that exist there. This flavorful

spice is fundamental to the regional economy and culture. The growth and production of vanilla beans can be learned about by taking guided tours of the farms that grow the spice. The air is thick with the aroma of vanilla, making for a lovely sensory experience.

3. Unspoiled Nature: Taha'a and Raiatea both offer unspoiled natural beauty. Rich valleys, gushing waterfalls, and breathtaking mountain peaks define Raiatea. The tranquil, remote beaches, coral gardens, and blue lagoons of Taha'a are well-known. These islands offer the chance to get close to nature by hiking, discovering secluded coves, or just lounging on the gorgeous beaches.

4. Water Activities: A wide range of water sports are perfect in the lagoons that surround Raiatea and Taha'a. Divers and snorkelers can swim with rays and tropical fish while exploring brilliant coral reefs and colorful marine life. Popular activities to take advantage of the tranquil seas

and discover the hidden treasures of the islands include sailing, kayaking, and paddleboarding.

5. Calm Ambiance: In contrast to busier tourist locations, Raiatea and Taha'a have a calm and relaxed atmosphere. These islands are ideal for anyone looking for a quiet getaway far from the masses. Luxurious resorts, romantic sunsets, and regional cuisine with fresh seafood and tropical flavors are all available for your relaxation.

Visits to Raiatea and Taha'a offer a special chance to learn about Polynesian culture, take in stunning natural scenery, and get a taste of the calm island way of life. These "Sacred Islands" provide an unforgettable and rewarding experience, whether you're looking for cultural exploration, outdoor adventures, or relaxation.

Huahine: French Polynesia's Undiscovered Gem

The alluring island of Huahine, often known as the "Hidden Gem" of French Polynesia, is renowned for its untainted beauty, extensive history, and serene atmosphere. Here are some reasons Huahine is special as a travel destination:

1. Genuine Polynesian Culture: Huahine provides a genuine look into everyday Polynesian life. The island has been successful in protecting its cultural history, and the inhabitants are proud of their traditions and way of life. By taking part in customary activities, going to cultural events, and visiting historical places, visitors may fully experience the island's vibrant Polynesian culture.

2. Natural Beauty: Huahine is endowed with pristine beauty. The island has pristine beaches, luxuriant tropical trees, and aquamarine lagoons.

Compared to other of the more well-known tourist locations in French Polynesia, it is less developed, allowing tourists to savor the tranquility of untamed nature. Hiking through deep rainforests, finding undiscovered waterfalls, and coming across unusual flora and fauna are all possible.

3. Historical Sites: Huahine is home to a number of ancient temples and archaeological sites that highlight its historical significance. Over 200 marae (traditional Polynesian temples) and other cultural landmarks can be found on the island. Huahine's history and cultural customs are explained by the Fare Pote'e Cultural Center. Additionally, you can see out the Maeva Archaeological Site, which has intact marae and other artifacts.

4. Adventures Off the Beaten Path Huahine provides a variety of adventures off the beaten path. By hiring a bike or scooter and traveling along the beautiful coastline roads, you may explore the island's various landscapes. Visit the

nearby motus (little islets) on a boat excursion, then enjoy lunches on isolated beaches. The island is a fantastic destination for fishermen because it is also renowned for having superb fishing.

5. Calm Beaches and Snorkeling Locations: The island of Huahine is home to several gorgeous beaches with silky white sand and crystal-clear turquoise water. Avea Beach, Hana Iti Beach, and Fare Beach are a few well-known beaches. These remote beaches provide peace and quiet as well as chances for swimming, picnics, and sunbathing. Divers and snorkelers can glimpse sea turtles while exploring colorful coral reefs and exotic fish.

6. Calm Ambiance: Huahine has a calm, easygoing atmosphere that makes it the perfect vacation spot for people looking to unwind and get away from the stress of daily life. The island's relaxed pace of life, welcoming residents, and natural surroundings provide a tranquil and restorative atmosphere.

You can venture off the main road and find French Polynesia's hidden treasures by traveling to Huahine. Huahine offers a singular and genuine experience that will charm you and make you wish to go back, from its rich cultural legacy to its unspoiled natural beauty.

The Marquesas Islands: Untouched and Far Away

French Polynesia's Marquesas Islands are a distant and largely unexplored archipelago that is located far from other popular tourist locations. The Marquesas Islands are regarded as a sanctuary for individuals seeking an adventure that is genuinely off the beaten path for the following reasons:

1. Remote Location: The Marquesas Islands are some of the world's most remote islands, located

in the South Pacific Ocean. They have been able to maintain its natural beauty and unique Polynesian culture thanks to their isolation. Visitors can expect an intense and personal experience due to the absence of mass tourism.

2. Unspoiled Natural Beauty: The Marquesas Islands are renowned for their stunning and rocky scenery. These islands are comprised of towering volcanic peaks, deep valleys, lush forests, gushing waterfalls, and quiet beaches. The Marquesas' pristine landscape provides fantastic chances for trekking, exploring, and getting in touch with the natural beauty of the surroundings.

3. Authentic Polynesian Culture: Polynesian history and culture are deeply ingrained in the Marquesas Islands. Locals are proud to show off their past to guests and have preserved their customs, crafts, and arts. Traditional dance performances, cultural events, and old archaeological sites, including stunning stone

tikis and me'ae (holy meeting places), are all available to see.

4. Antiquated Archaeological Sites: The Marquesas Islands are home to an impressive array of antiquated sites, some of which date back thousands of years. Massive stone tikis may be seen in locations like the Valley of the Kings on Hiva Oa and the Puamau Tiki Site on Hiva Oa, which serve as examples of the Marquesan people's exceptional craftsmanship and religious convictions.

5. Genuine Cuisine: The Marquesas Islands provide a special dining experience with an emphasis on authentic Polynesian fare. You can enjoy local specialties like poisson cru (raw fish marinated in coconut milk), breadfruit-based dishes, and other cuisines. The island's reliance on natural resources is reflected in the cuisine's genuine flavors and freshness.

6. Outdoor Adventures: The Marquesas Islands' isolation offers a wealth of outdoor adventure

activities. To find quiet waterfalls, hidden valleys, and panoramic overlooks, you can set out on strenuous hikes. Additionally, you may enjoy the abundant marine life and clear waterways around the islands by snorkeling, diving, fishing, and going on boat trips.

A visit to a secluded and unspoiled paradise is the Marquesas Islands. These islands provide visitors looking for an off-the-beaten-path journey with a distinctive and genuine experience, from the breathtaking landscapes to the colorful Polynesian culture. It's important to keep in mind that due to the islands' isolated location, transit options, lodging options, and service options may be limited, so it's best to plan and reserve ahead of time.

When to visit Tahiti and Bora Bora

The dry season, which typically lasts from May to October, is the ideal time to visit Tahiti, Bora Bora, and other islands in French Polynesia. This time of year is perfect for outdoor activities and taking in the natural beauty of the islands because there is less rain, less humidity, and warmer temperatures.

When organizing your visit, keep the following things in mind:

1. Climate: Temperatures throughout the dry season range from the mid-70s°F (mid-20s°C) to the mid-80s°F (about 30°C), and are generally consistent and pleasant. This time of year is more comfortable for outdoor exploration and aquatic sports because the humidity is reduced.

2. Crowds: The islands may be busier during the dry season than during other times of the year because it also happens to be the busiest travel period. If you prefer a more sedate and uncrowded experience, you can think about going in April or November, when the weather is still pleasant but there are less people.

3. High Season: Due to school breaks, the months of July and August are regarded as the high season, particularly for travelers from Europe and North America. During this time, it's best to reserve lodging and activities far in advance because supply could be scarce.

4. Whale viewing: If whale viewing is something you're interested in, schedule your trip between July and October. You have a better chance of spotting humpback whales during this time, especially in Moorea and Bora Bora. They are migrating to the waters of French Polynesia.

5. Tropical Showers: Although the dry season often sees less rainfall, it's important to

remember that French Polynesia can have sporadic tropical showers all year long. However, these showers typically pass quickly and are followed by clear skies.

6. Off-Season Advantages: Traveling to Tahiti and Bora Bora from November to April might have benefits including lower lodging costs and fewer people. It's crucial to keep in mind that because this time frame occurs during the wet season, you can experience more frequent rain and greater humidity levels.

The ideal time to travel to Tahiti and Bora Bora ultimately depends on your priorities and interests. To get the most out of your visit to these magnificent islands, make sure to plan ahead and take into account variables like the weather, crowds, and particular activities you want to engage in.

Visa requirements and necessary travel papers

Depending on your country and the reason for your trip, you may need a visa and other travel documentation to visit Tahiti, Bora Bora, and other French Polynesian islands. Here are some general details to help you comprehend the prerequisites:

1. Visa Exemption: Many nationals, including those from the United States, Canada, the United Kingdom, and the majority of the European Union, are exempt from needing a visa to visit French Polynesia. They are permitted admission without a visa for periods of up to 90 days. The particular visa requirements for your place of citizenship should be confirmed, though, as they are subject to change.

2. Passport Validity: Make sure your passport will remain valid for at least six months after the

date you intend to leave French Polynesia. The majority of nationalities are subject to this rule.

3. Return or Onward Ticket: Depending on the circumstances, you might be required to show a return or onward ticket upon arrival to prove that you intend to depart French Polynesia within the allotted time frame.

4. Entry and Departure Forms: Upon arrival, you will need to fill out an immigration form with basic details about your identity and itinerary. A copy of this form should be saved because you'll need it to leave French Polynesia.

5. Extended Stays: If you intend to stay in French Polynesia for a period of time longer than 90 days or if your visit is for a different reason—such as job, school, or family reunion—you may need to apply for the necessary visas or permits before traveling there. For comprehensive information on visa requirements specific to your situation, get in

touch with the French embassy or consulate nearest you.

In light of the fact that visa and entry requirements are subject to change, it is advised to check with the French embassy or consulate in your area or to visit the French Polynesian government's official website for the most recent and accurate information.

Additionally, it is strongly advised to purchase travel insurance to cover any unanticipated occurrences or emergencies while visiting Tahiti and Bora Bora.

Exchange of money and currency

The French Pacific Franc (XPF) is the official currency of French Polynesia, which includes Tahiti and Bora Bora. Here are some details on currency and exchange rates in the area:

1. French Pacific Franc (XPF): The French Pacific Franc's currency code is XPF, and it is frequently represented by the letters "F" or "CFP." The currency has a fixed exchange rate that is tied to the euro.

2. money Availability: The French Pacific Franc is the main unit of money in French Polynesia. In hotels, restaurants, shops, and other tourist attractions, it is commonly accepted. For smaller businesses, neighborhood markets, and distant locations where credit card acceptance may be constrained, it's a good idea to have some cash.

3. Money Exchange: In big cities like Papeete (the capital of Tahiti), money can be exchanged at banks, post offices, and currency exchange offices. While other hotels and resorts might also provide currency exchange services, the rates might not be as good. To get the greatest value, it's a good idea to compare exchange rates and costs. Remember that services for exchanging currencies could only be partially available on weekends and holidays.

4. ATMs and Credit Cards: French Polynesia's major towns and cities have easy access to ATMs (automated teller machines). You can use your debit or credit card to get cash in the local currency from them. American Express and Diners Club may be accepted to a lesser extent than Visa and Mastercard. To prevent any problems with card transactions, let your bank or credit card issuer know about your vacation intentions.

5. Traveler's checks: These are uncommon in French Polynesia and may only be accepted in certain circumstances. For convenience, it is advised to carry a combination of cash and credit/debit cards.

6. Tipping: Since a 10% service charge is sometimes tacked on to the bill, tipping is not a prevalent practice in French Polynesia. However, if you would like to give a little gratuity for really good service, that is appreciated.

To be prepared for emergencies and little purchases, it is a good idea to carry some local cash. To get the greatest deal while transferring money, be aware of charges and exchange rates.

Tips for health and safety

Your health and safety should come first when visiting Tahiti, Bora Bora, or any other French Polynesian location. Here are some crucial health and safety advice to take into account:

1. Travel insurance: Before departing, be certain you have complete travel insurance that covers medical costs, trip cancellation/interruption, and any other potential dangers. Check your policy to see what is covered, and have a copy of your insurance information on you at all times.

2. immunizations: Make sure you are up to date on standard immunizations by consulting your doctor or a travel clinic well in advance.

Depending on your particular travel intentions and medical history, they might also suggest extra immunizations or preventive measures.

3. Sun Protection: Because French Polynesia has intense UV radiation, it's important to use sun protection. Wear sunglasses, a wide-brimmed hat, protective clothes, and sunscreen with a high SPF. During the hottest times of the day, seek shade and stay hydrated.

4. Mosquito Protection: Take precautions against mosquitoes, which can spread diseases including dengue fever and the Zika virus. Wear long sleeves and pants, use DEET-containing insect repellents, and if required, think about sleeping under a mosquito net.

5. Hygiene and Water Safety: Wash your hands frequently with soap and water, especially before eating, to maintain good hygiene. Avoid consuming raw or undercooked food and instead opt to drink bottled or properly treated water.

Make sure the food is cooked and served hot when purchasing it from street sellers.

6. Traveler's diarrhea: Unless you can peel them yourself, stay away from tap water, ice cubes, raw fruits and vegetables, and unpeeled produce. Limit yourself to cooked meals from recognized restaurants and bottled water.

7. Water Activities: If you intend to participate in water sports like swimming, snorkeling, or diving, make sure you have the requisite knowledge and adhere to safety precautions. Use appropriate safety gear and only partake in water activities with reputed operators.

8. Emergency Services: Learn the local emergency phone numbers and the locations of the hospitals in your area. Make immediate contact with the appropriate authorities or seek medical help if necessary.

To ensure a safe and pleasurable journey, keep in mind to exercise caution, be on the lookout, and take the required safety precautions. It's always a good idea to keep up with the most recent travel warnings and get particular health and safety advice before your trip from medical professionals or government sources.

Language and Interaction

French is French Polynesia's official language. However, English is also frequently used, particularly in resorts, hotels, and tourist hotspots. Following are some things to keep in mind when communicating in Tahiti, Bora Bora, and other French Polynesian islands:

1. French Language: It can be useful to learn a few simple French words before traveling to French Polynesia, or to carry a pocket-sized French phrasebook. This can help you in routine interactions like saying hello to neighbors, placing a meal order, getting directions, or going shopping.

2. English is widely spoken in resort areas, hotels, and popular tourist destinations. English proficiency is common among natives employed in the tourism sector, including tour guides, hotel personnel, and restaurant staff. However, people's levels of English proficiency can vary, especially in more rural or less visited areas.

3. Polynesian Languages: Local residents also speak the Polynesian languages of Tahitian and Maohi (Marquesan), in addition to French and English. Even while you might not need to learn these languages for everyday conversation, acquiring a few Tahitian words and phrases might help you appreciate the language and integrate into the community.

4. Communication Advice: It's customary to say "Bonjour" (hello) or "Ia ora na" (a traditional greeting from Tahiti) and "Merci" (thank you) when speaking with locals. Positive encounters are greatly facilitated by politeness and friendliness.

5. Translation Apps: You can use translation apps on your smartphone or carry a pocket-sized language translation device if you're worried about linguistic difficulties. You can use these tools to communicate and comprehend common words and phrases in several languages.

6. Cultural Sensitivity: Although language can serve as a conduit for communication, it's crucial to respect regional norms and traditions and to be aware of cultural variations. Building strong relationships will be facilitated by your sensitivity to and appreciation for the Polynesian culture's emphasis on respect, family, and community.

Overall, even though English is widely used in tourist regions, French Polynesia's official language is French. Your relationships will be improved and your trip will be more enjoyable if you are polite and willing to learn a few simple phrases.

Local cuisine and Cultural Etiquette

It's crucial to understand the customs and food of the French Polynesian islands when traveling to Tahiti, Bora Bora, and other locales. Here are some pointers to assist you respect cultural customs and take advantage of the cuisine:

Cultural Manners:

1. Greetings: The Polynesians value greetings highly. It's normal to smile and say "Ia ora na" (a traditional Tahitian greeting) or "Bonjour" (a traditional French greeting) when meeting someone. The traditional way for friends and acquaintances to greet each other is with a kiss on each cheek.

2. Respect for Elders: Respect for elders is important in Polynesian culture. Maintain proper levels of respect and deference when conversing with senior citizens.

3. Modest Dress: Because Polynesian culture is typically conservative, it is best to dress modestly, especially when visiting villages, temples, or other places of worship. If you're at a beach or resort, you should wear swimwear; otherwise, you should cover yourself.

4. Taking Off Your Shoes: It's normal to take off your shoes before entering a person's home, a traditional gathering place (marae), or some establishments, like quaint stores or eateries. If there are a lot of shoes at the entry, for example, look for signs that you should take yours off.

5. Respect for the Environment and the Land: In French Polynesia, the environment and the land are highly revered. Avoid destroying coral reefs, disturbing wildlife, or littering to demonstrate your regard for the environment. During eco-tours or outdoor activities, adhere to any rules or instructions given.

Regional cuisine

1. Traditional foods: Try traditional Polynesian foods to get a taste of the native fare. Popular meals include fafaru (fermented fish or seafood), poisson cru (raw fish marinated in lime and coconut milk), taro root dishes, and breadfruit dishes.

2. Seafood: The fresh seafood in French Polynesia is renowned. Take advantage of the profusion of fish, such as tuna, mahi-mahi, and parrotfish, as well as the delectable lobster and prawns in the shellfish category.

3. Poi: A mainstay of Polynesian cuisine, poi is a starchy paste prepared from taro root. Due to its unusual texture, it is frequently served with other meals and might be a challenge to like.

4. Local Fruits: Snack on French Polynesia's tropical fruits like papaya, pineapple, mango, coconut, and passion fruit. These fruits are

frequently offered either raw or in a light fruit salad.

5. Food Festivals: Keep an eye out for local markets or food festivals where you can enjoy a range of regional specialties. These occasions are a wonderful way to get a taste of the islands' thriving culinary scene.

Never be afraid to ask locals where to get the greatest local cuisine, and always be open to trying new flavors and culinary experiences.

You can immerse yourself in French Polynesia's rich cultural heritage and enhance your trip by practicing local rituals with respect and sampling the delectable local cuisine.

Polynesian Traditions and Culture

Tahiti, Bora Bora, and other nearby islands in French Polynesia are home to a vibrant polynesian culture. To understand and respect the way of life in the region, consider the following significant elements of Polynesian culture and customs:

1. Oral Traditions: Storytelling, chants, and songs play a crucial role in maintaining history, folklore, and cultural values in Polynesian culture. The cultural legacy of the islands is frequently celebrated by showcasing traditional performances like hula and drum dances.

2. Honoring Elders: The Polynesians have a deep regard for their elders. It is traditional to respect elders in the family and in the community and to ask their advice. It is highly

regarded to address them with appropriate titles and express appreciation for their insight and understanding.

3. Community and Family: In Polynesian culture, the idea of an extended family and community is crucial. Family ties are strong, and numerous generations frequently participate in gatherings and festivities. People are motivated to contribute to the community's well-being because it is highly respected and appreciated.

4. Tapu (sanctity): The sense of sanctity and regard for particular locations, items, and traditions is referred to as tapu. Respect should be shown for any manifestations of tapu, such as sacred places (marae), graveyards, or customary practices. If you are unsure about any specific tapu-related practices, ask the local authorities or community members for permission or advice.

5. Craftsmanship and Art: Polynesians are renowned for their skill and aesthetic expression. French Polynesia is known for its intricate wood

carvings, woven goods, and native tattoos (tatau). These artistic mediums frequently feature symbolic depictions of myths, deities, and the natural world.

6. Connection to Nature: Polynesians have a strong sense of belonging to nature and a great respect for both the land and the sea. It is reflected in traditional activities including fishing, farming, and travel. To preserve the fragile balance between humans and nature, sustainable practices and resource conservation are prioritized.

7. Polynesian Tattoos: In Polynesian culture, tattoos have special meaning. Tatau or moko, which are traditional tattoos, are elaborate designs with symbolic meanings. They frequently show histories, ancestry, and tribal affiliations. Tattoos are regarded as a form of self-expression and as a method to stay connected to one's history.

8. Hospitality and Sharing: The warmth and generosity of Polynesian hospitality are well known. Visitors are frequently received with open arms and shown genuine courtesy. Polynesian culture places a high value on sharing meals, tales, and experiences, and it is traditional to express gratitude for this hospitality.

It's crucial to respect and appreciate the local culture when traveling to French Polynesia. Keep an eye out for and pick up on the cultural customs of others around you, and interact with them in a cordial and courteous way. You can better comprehend the rich history and traditions of the islands by embracing Polynesian customs.

Traditional Arts and Crafts

Traditional arts and crafts are an important component of French Polynesia's cultural history and play a key role in Polynesian culture. When visiting Tahiti, Bora Bora, and other nearby islands, keep reading to learn about and admire some examples of local arts and crafts:

1. Wood Carving: In French Polynesia, wood carving is a highly regarded art form. Using a variety of woods, including tropical hardwoods, skilled artisans carve and sculpt beautiful works of art. In traditional carvings, deities, ancestors, animals, or geometric patterns are frequently shown. These carvings are typically seen on ornamental items, ceremonial masks, or finely carved house posts.

2. Weaving: In Polynesian culture, weaving is a significant craft as well. Baskets, mats, caps, and other useful objects are frequently made from palm leaves, pandanus, and coconut fronds. Using age-old methods that have been handed down through the years, intricate designs and patterns are woven. These woven objects have cultural and symbolic importance in addition to being useful.

3. Tapa Cloth: In Polynesia, "tapa" or "siapo" are terms for the traditional fabric fashioned from the paper mulberry tree's bark. Bark is beaten, layered, and dyed by artisans to produce soft, enduring cloth with distinctive patterns and designs. Tapa cloth is used for ceremonial purposes, wall hangings, and apparel.

4. Pearl jewelry: Tahitian pearls, which are gorgeous black pearls, are famously produced in French Polynesia. Pearls are expertly harvested and grown by local craftspeople, who frequently craft them into exquisite jewelry. Tahitian pearl bracelets, necklaces, and earrings are in high demand and make lovely gifts.

5. Tattoos (Tatau): Polynesian tattoos, sometimes referred to as tatau or moko, are a traditional type of body art with significant cultural and personal meanings. Intricate and significant designs that reflect a person's identity, family history, and cultural symbols are made using traditional tattooing techniques. This revered practice is carried on by tattoo artists in French

Polynesia, and obtaining a Polynesian tattoo can be a means to be in touch with the community.

6. Shell products: In Polynesian culture, shells have special cultural value. Local artisans use a variety of shells to make exquisite products. Popular crafts include shell necklaces, bracelets, earrings, and decorative objects. The relationship between Polynesians and the ocean is reflected in these crafts, which frequently use traditional motifs.

Discovering and acquiring traditional arts and crafts not only helps the local economy but also enables you to take a piece of Polynesian craftsmanship and culture back home. Look for genuine crafts produced by regional makers while making purchases, and find out the histories and cultural value of each item.

Tahiti cuisine: Regional dishes and Ingredients

Tahitian food is a delicious blend of French and Polynesian ingredients. Tahiti's cuisine makes the most of the plentiful fresh fish, exotic fruits, and locally produced resources. Check out these traditional Tahitian foods and ingredients:

1. Poisson Cru: The national dish of Tahiti and a must-try. This meal is created with raw fish, usually tuna or mahi-mahi, marinated in lime juice and coconut milk. It is a light, refreshing dish. Salt and pepper are frequently added, and it is frequently combined with onions, tomatoes, and cucumbers. A wonderful flavor is produced by blending the flavors of citrus and coconut.

2. Fafa: Taro leaves are used to make this traditional Tahitian delicacy. After being blanched, the leaves are cooked with coconut milk, onions, garlic, and occasionally pig or

chicken. As a result, a creamy and tasty side or main entrée is created.

3. Po'e: Made from mashed fruits like bananas or papayas and thickened with cornstarch, po'e is a typical Tahitian dessert. It is flavored with vanilla or coconut milk and sweetened with sugar. Usually eaten with a coconut milk sauce or topped with shredded coconut, po'e is steamed or baked.

4. Marinated Pork or Chicken: Tahitian cuisine includes meats grilled over an open flame that have been marinated. A blend of lime juice, soy sauce, garlic, ginger, and other spices is frequently used to marinade chicken or pig. The meat is then expertly grilled to produce tender and tasty dishes.

5. Breadfruit: Tahitian cuisine frequently uses breadfruit as an ingredient. This fruit is starchy and can be boiled, roasted, or fried. It is frequently used as a side dish or as a potato alternative. Additionally, breadfruit can be

turned into a paste known as "ma'a" and used in a variety of conventional cuisines.

Tahiti is endowed with an abundance of tropical fruits, which is number six. Enjoy the flavors of luscious papayas, sweet pineapples, juicy mangoes, aromatic bananas, and tart passion fruit. These fruits are frequently eaten raw, as fruit salads, or as side dishes with meals.

7. Tahiti is renowned for its premium vanilla. Warm weather and rich soil on the islands result in vanilla beans with a distinctive flowery and delicious flavor. Tahitian vanilla is frequently used in ice cream, sweets, pastries, and blended into a variety of drinks.

8. Seafood: Tahitian cuisine highlights a vast range of seafood due to the island nation's abundant marine resources. Tuna, mahi-mahi, and parrotfish are popular examples of fresh fish. Additionally popular are prawns, lobsters, and other shellfish. Seafood meals that are

grilled, cooked, or covered with sauces bring out the inherent flavors of the ocean.

Be sure to check out the neighborhood markets and eateries to try the vivacious and savory Tahitian food when you travel to Tahiti and other French Polynesian islands. Discover how Tahitian cuisine is a great gourmet joy thanks to its distinctive combination of tropical ingredients, traditional cooking methods, and cultural influences.

Dining and Drinking Spots

There are several dining options in Tahiti and Bora Bora that can accommodate visitors with various tastes and preferences. Here are some well-known places you can check out:

1. Roulottes: Common in Tahiti, especially in Papeete, roulottes are food trucks or mobile food kiosks. These vivacious food trucks serve a variety of regional and international fare,

including as crepes, grilled meats, Chinese food, and Tahitian delicacies like poisson cru and other fish. In addition to being a terrific choice for inexpensive and excellent meals, roulottes frequently make for a vibrant scene in the evenings.

2. Resort restaurants: Tahiti and Bora Bora are both home to a number of opulent resorts, many of which provide top-notch dining options. Many of these resorts feature numerous dining establishments that offer French, Polynesian, and other cuisines. Resort dining establishments are renowned for their exquisite waterfront views, premium ingredients, and inventive presentation.

3. Local Snack Bars: Keep an eye out for tiny neighborhood "snack bars" or "snacks" that serve quick and reasonably priced meals. These informal restaurants offer a wide range of food, including sandwiches, burgers, and snacks like frites (French fries), as well as plate lunches with grilled meats, rice, and salad. Both residents and

tourists enjoy snack bars because they provide them a taste of traditional Tahitian cuisine.

4. Beachfront eateries: Tahiti and Bora Bora's magnificent beaches and lagoons allow many eateries to take advantage of their prime locations. There are restaurants on the beach where you may eat with your toes in the sand and savor a variety of fresh seafood, grilled delicacies, and tropical drinks.

5. Local Patisseries: Tahiti's pastry culture is clearly influenced by France. A delicious selection of French pastries, bread, and cakes are available at patisseries or bakeries. Enjoy a cup of flavorful coffee or tea with croissants, pain au chocolat, macarons, and other delicious sweets.

6. Bars and Lounge spaces: Tahiti and Bora Bora both feature bars and lounge spaces where you can unwind with tropical cocktails, local beers, or foreign spirits. To improve the mood, some restaurants provide live music or cultural performances.

7. Food Tours and Experiences: Enroll in food tours or cooking classes to really immerse yourself in Tahitian cuisine. You can learn about regional ingredients, connect with merchants, explore local markets, and take part in cooking demonstrations to make your own Tahitian delicacies through these experiences.

Don't forget to sample regional cuisine and experience Tahiti and Bora Bora's flavors, whether at well-known restaurants or undiscovered spots that locals suggest. Asking hotel employees, tour guides, or locals for recommendations is a great way to find the best restaurants while you're there.

Here are a few well-known eateries in Tahiti and Bora Bora:

Restaurants in Tahiti:

1. Le Coco's Restaurant - Papeete
2. Le Lotus - Papeete
3. Les Roulottes de Papeete - Papeete (food trucks)
4. Le Carré - Papeete

5. L'O à la Bouche - Papeete
6. La Villa Mahana - Papeete
7. Restaurant Le Belvédère - Pirae
8. Le Bistrot - Papeete
9. Le Coco Beach - Punaauia
10. Le Royal Tahitien - Pirae

Restaurants in Bora Bora:
1. Bloody Mary's - Bora Bora
2. Villa Mahana - Bora Bora
3. St. James Bora Bora - Bora Bora
4. Le Tipanié - Bora Bora
5. Lagoon by Jean-Georges - Bora Bora
6. Matira Beach Restaurant - Bora Bora
7. Kaina Hut - Bora Bora
8. Bora Bora Yacht Club - Bora Bora
9. La Villa Mahana - Bora Bora
10. Fare Manuia - Bora Bora

It is important to keep in mind that restaurant availability and popularity might change over time, so it is always a good idea to check recent reviews and suggestions before going.

Overwater bungalows and upscale resorts

Famous for their breathtaking natural beauty and opulent resorts, Tahiti and Bora Bora are known for their overwater bungalows, which provide an unforgettable experience. The following list of Tahiti and Bora Bora's top luxury resorts and overwater bungalows includes:

One of the best resorts in Bora Bora is The St. Regis Bora Bora Resort, which offers large overwater villas with private pools and easy access to the clear lagoon. provides butler service, a full-service spa, a variety of dining options, and breath-taking Mount Otemanu views.

2. Four Seasons Resort Bora Bora, in the South Pacific island of Bora Bora, is renowned for its opulent overwater bungalows and beachfront

villas with private plunge pools. provides a variety of water sports, a holistic spa, exquisite dining options, and breathtaking lagoon views.

3. InterContinental Bora Bora Resort & Thalasso Spa (Bora Bora): - Provides environmentally responsible overwater villas with private sundecks and glass flooring for viewing marine life.
   - Offers a gorgeous coral garden, numerous dining options, and an award-winning spa.

4. The Tetiaroa Brando: This eco-luxury resort is situated on a private island and provides quiet overwater villas with private plunge pools. well-known for its environmental initiatives, immaculate beaches, and water sports including kayaking, paddleboarding, and snorkeling.

5. Taha'a's Le Taha'a Island Resort & Spa:
   This resort, which is located on a private motu, provides opulent overwater suites with roomy terraces and stunning views. features access to

Taha'a's vanilla-scented landscapes, a peaceful spa, and food with Polynesian influences.

6. Conrad Bora Bora Nui (Bora Bora): - Provides roomy beachfront bedrooms and overwater villas with private pools and expansive views. offers a variety of water activities, a hilltop spa, a variety of restaurants, and an exquisite infinity pool.

7. Pearl Resorts' Le Bora Bora

8. International Bora Bora IHG hotel Le Moana Resort

9. Maui Polynesia Bora Bora

10. The Le Meridien in Bora Bora

11. Hotel Eden Beach in Bora Bora

The opulent resorts and overwater bungalows that may be found in Tahiti and Bora Bora are just a few examples. Every resort in this tropical paradise has its own distinctive characteristics and amenities, guaranteeing a wonderful and enjoyable stay.

Boutique inns and lodgings

-Matira Hotel
Wooden bungalows with simple furnishings in a laid-back coastal hotel with a restaurant and grounds.
-Maitai Polynesia Hotel
Simple seaside hotel with two relaxed restaurants, two pubs, and free canoes and kayaks.
-Bounty Lodge Rangiroa | French Polynesian Boutique Hotel
-Pension Alice et Raphael Bora-Bora -Hotel Royal Bora Bora
Unhurried family-run B&B with kayaks available for loan and basic, eco-chic cottages on a secluded beach.
-Bora Bora Marara Beach Resort, Sofitel
High-end resort including a spa, a pool, and luxurious villas and bungalows, some with direct access to the ocean.
-The Pearl of Taha
-Matira Hotel

Wooden bungalows with simple furnishings in a laid-back coastal hotel with a restaurant and grounds.

Affordable Accommodations

- Sundown Hill Inn
Unpretentious guesthouse featuring vibrant studios and apartments, lagoon views, and a free airport shuttle.
-Maitai Polynesia Hotel
Simple seaside hotel with two relaxed restaurants, two pubs, and free canoes and kayaks.
Budget-wise, it's the ideal location for fully experiencing Bora Bora.
-Royal Bora Hotel Bora
Unpretentious hotel featuring a private beach, outdoor pool, and thatched-roof restaurant.
"Really good value for the added quality"
-Alice and Raphael Bora-Bora Pension

Unhurried family-run B&B with kayaks available for loan and basic, eco-chic cottages on a secluded beach.

-Holiday's Lodge & Villa in Bora Bora

Simple accommodations with warm bungalows are available in a relaxed hotel with gardens, a pool, and views of the lagoon.

-The Pearl of Taha

Choosing the Best Accommodation Location

There are a few things to think about while deciding on the ideal location for your vacation in Tahiti and Bora Bora. French Polynesia's Tahiti and Bora Bora are both breathtaking locations, yet they provide slightly distinct experiences. Here is a guide to assist you in making a knowledgeable choice:

The largest and most populated island in French Polynesia is Tahiti, which also serves as the region's entry point. It combines beautiful natural scenery with metropolitan regions.

- Consider vacationing in Papeete, the capital of Tahiti, if you want a lively city atmosphere with a variety of lodging options, dining establishments, and nightlife. Explore other parts of the island for a more calm and private experience, such as the opulent resorts on Tahiti's west coast (such Punaauia) or the serene beaches of Tahiti Iti (the smaller peninsula).

- Tahiti also provides opportunity for waterfall exploration, botanical garden visits, trekking, and getting immersed in Polynesian culture.

2. Bora Bora: Known for its distinctive overwater bungalows, gorgeous blue lagoon, and immaculate white-sand beaches, Bora Bora is a popular vacation destination. It is regarded as a charming and opulent vacation spot.

- Bora Bora is a great option if you're looking for a picture-perfect paradise where you can relax, indulge in water sports, and stay in opulent resorts.

- The majority of the upscale resorts are located around the main island, which is the primary spot to stay in Bora Bora. Numerous of them have easy access to the lagoon as well as a range of extras like spa services, diving, and snorkeling.

- An alternative option that offers a more secluded and private experience is to stay on a smaller motu (islet) that surrounds the main island.

Budget: Although Tahiti and Bora Bora are known for their upscale resorts, there are also more moderately priced options available. Examine the range of rooms available in each location while keeping your budget in mind.

- Activities: Consider the pursuits you'd like to make. Tahiti offers a wider variety of activities, such as trekking, cultural immersion, and city exploration. The emphasis on relaxation and water sports is greater in Bora Bora.

- Accessibility: Tahiti offers greater international flight connections than Bora Bora, despite both islands having airports. Start your vacation in

Tahiti and then move on to Bora Bora if you prefer simpler access.

The decision between Tahiti and Bora Bora ultimately comes down to your preferences and the kind of experience you're looking for. To ensure a memorable and pleasurable stay in French Polynesia, take into account the criteria outlined above and make the necessary plans.

Family-friendly Activities and Traveling Advice

Certainly! Here are some broad ideas for family-friendly activities and travel advice:

Family-friendly activities include the following:
1. Visit an amusement park or theme park. Many locations have amusement parks or theme parks that provide entertainment for visitors of all ages. Choose parks based on your family's interests and age range after conducting research.

2. Discover Nature: Arrange outdoor activities like picnics, hikes, and nature walks in parks or nature reserves. This enables your family to exercise together, enjoy the outdoors, and connect with nature.

3. Visit interactive displays and activities at museums and scientific centers that are geared toward kids. The entire family may enjoy these locations while learning something new.

4. Animal Encounters: Children may view and learn about various animal species by visiting zoos, aquariums, and wildlife refuges. For kids' excitement, some places even let them interact with or feed the animals.

5. Visit Cultural and Historical Sites: Look around the local historical and cultural monuments and sites. This can be a wonderful opportunity to expose your kids to various countries, traditions, and historical periods.

6. Outdoor Sports and Recreation: Play sports like soccer or frisbee, go biking, go boating, go fishing, or engage in other outdoor sports and recreation. These pursuits foster physical wellness and foster enjoyable family interactions.

Family travel advice:
1. Work together to research and plan: Include your family in the planning process for your trip. Choose vacation spots, activities, and sites that everyone will love after discussion. Each member of the family will have something to anticipate as a result.

2. Make a list of the important stuff and pack wisely from it. Take into account each family member's needs, including those for clothing, medications, entertainment, and any particular items needed for the scheduled activities.

3. Select family-friendly lodging: Seek out family-friendly lodgings, such as inns or resorts with facilities like kid-friendly pools, play areas,

and kids' clubs. For larger families, connecting rooms or suites can be the best option.

4. Maintain a Flexible Schedule: Make room in your schedule for rest, meals, and unforeseen delays. Do not overbook yourself because this can cause stress and weariness.

5. Keep Safety a Priority: Make sure everyone in your family is safe by being familiar with the local emergency protocols. With your kids, go over safety guidelines and decide on meeting places in case someone gets lost.

6. Capture and Record Memories: To record your family's adventures, take pictures, make movies, or even start a travel journal. In order to generate enduring memories, encourage your kids to take part in the trip's documentation.

Remember that every family is different, so customize these games and suggestions to fit the interests, ages, and preferences of your own family. Have fun on your family vacations!

Beaches and attractions geared toward kids

Famous for their amazing beauty and magnificent beaches are the islands of Tahiti and Bora Bora. Despite being frequently linked with romance getaways, there are several family-friendly beaches and attractions. In Tahiti and Bora Bora, the following beaches and attractions are suggested as family-friendly:

1. Plage de Maui: This well-liked family-friendly beach is situated on Tahiti's west coast. It's a wonderful place for kids to swim and play because of the calm waves and nice sand. Families can unwind at picnic spaces and shady locations.

2. Maraa Grotto: Situated in Tahiti's beautiful valleys, the Maraa Grotto is a natural cave that kids will adore exploring. There are numerous

swimming-safe, clear freshwater pools throughout the grotto. The entire family will enjoy this unusual and exciting event.

1.Matira Beach is the most well-known beach in Bora Bora and a fantastic choice for families. For kids to play and swim in, the waters are shallow and transparent. Additionally, there are hotels and dining establishments lining the shore, offering family-friendly services.

2. Bora Bora Lagoonarium: Bora Bora also boasts a lagoonarium, similar to the one in Tahiti. Kids can watch and engage with a variety of marine animals, including tropical fish, rays, and even sharks (in a supervised environment), by snorkeling or going on a glass-bottom boat trip.

3. Turtle Center: The Turtle Center is a sea turtle sanctuary that is situated in Le Meridien Bora Bora. Families may go see these interesting species and learn about them, and kids can even

help feed the animals. For kids, it's a worthwhile educational and memorable experience.

Please be advised that as things might change over time, it's always a good idea to check with local authorities or your hotel for the most recent information on the accessibility and safety of these attractions.

Family-friendly accommodations and features

In order to make sure that families with children have a pleasant and happy vacation, Tahiti and Bora Bora both provide a variety of family-friendly resorts and amenities. Here are some alternatives to think about:

Tahiti offers a number of family-friendly features, such as roomy apartments or bungalows, a swimming pool, and a kids' club with supervised activities. On request, they also offer cribs and babysitter services.

2. Le Meridien Tahiti: Lc Meridien offers roomy family suites and rooms, as well as a kids' center and a pool for little ones. They plan a variety of kid-friendly events, including sports, games, and arts and crafts.

3. Manava Suite Resort Tahiti: Offering family suites with separate bedrooms and sitting areas, Manava Suite Resort gives plenty of accommodation for families. There includes a swimming pool, a kids' pool, and a kids' club where youngsters can engage in activities under adult supervision.

1. Four Seasons Resort in Bora Bora Family-friendly lodging options are available in the opulent overwater bungalows and beachfront villas at Bora Bora. They offer free children's amenities including high chairs, baby cots, and kid-sized toiletries. A kids' club and a teen

center with a variety of activities are also available at the resort.

Family-friendly overwater villas with separate bedrooms and living areas are available at the InterContinental Bora Bora Resort & Thalasso Spa. They have a playground, a kid's pool, and a kids' club. On request, the resort also offers childcare services.

3. Bora Bora Pearl Beach Resort & Spa: This resort has beachfront villas with private pools and family rooms. They have a kids' pool and a kids' club with supervised activities. Additionally, the resort provides free kayaks and snorkeling gear for family aquatic experiences.

Only a few resorts in Tahiti and Bora Bora are suitable for families. It's usually a good idea to verify the precise amenities and services provided by each resort before making travel arrangements to make sure they suit your family's requirements and preferences.

Traveling with Children: Some Advice

Although it necessitates additional planning and preparation, traveling with kids can be a fun and rewarding experience. Here are some suggestions to make your family's trip easier and more pleasurable:

1. Research your trip in advance to identify amenities, attractions, and activities geared toward children. Make a list of must-see locations and a flexible plan that takes into consideration your children's needs and interests.

2. Pack Smartly: Place necessary goods in your carry-on bag, like diapers, wipes, food, and additional clothing. To keep kids occupied on the trip, don't forget to pack entertainment options like books, toys, and electronics.

3. Select family-friendly lodging: Look for lodgings that welcome families with young children. Think about things like room size, childproofing alternatives, and the presence of amenities like playgrounds, swimming pools, and kids' clubs.

4. Be Aware of Jet Lag: If you're crossing time zones, be aware that you may have jet lag. A few days before the trip, change your kids' sleep schedule, make sure they're well-hydrated on the plane, and work to get them into a new habit as soon as possible after you arrive.

5. Pace Yourself and Take Breaks: Children may require periodic rest breaks, so make sure to factor that into your schedule. Give them plenty of time to recover, and incorporate activities that are tailored to their interests and energy levels.

6. Include Children in the Planning Process: Give your kids a say in the journey arrangements. Engage them in decision-making and give them the freedom to select the

attractions or activities that interest them. They will remain interested and involved as a result throughout the journey.

7. Be Patient and Flexible: Keep in mind that traveling with kids might occasionally be unpredictable. Be ready for unforeseen delays, temper outbursts, or plan modifications. Keep an upbeat mindset, be adaptable, and be patient when facing problems.

8. Ensure Safety: Always put your kids' safety first. Use safety harnesses or wristbands if necessary, keep a tight check on them in crowded areas, and teach them the fundamental travel safety guidelines like not chatting to strangers and sticking near to you in unexpected locations.

9. Permit Cultural Immersion: Encourage your kids to take part in the local customs and traditions while you're traveling. Visit regional markets, sample regional cuisine, and take part

in cultural activities suitable for children. The entire family may enjoy and learn from this.

10. Capture Memories: Document your family's trips with numerous images to preserve the memories. Give your kids disposable cameras or let them use their own gadgets (if age-appropriate) to take pictures of the vacation.

Always keep in mind that family time and shared experiences can be had while traveling with kids. Accept the challenge and have fun traveling together!

websites for making reservations for excursions, activities, and lodging.

The following are some well-known websites for making reservations for travel, leisure, and lodging:
1. Booking.com (www.booking.com)
2. Expedia (www.expedia.com)

3. Airbnb (www.airbnb.com)
4. TripAdvisor (www.tripadvisor.com)
5. Viator (www.viator.com)
6. Kayak (www.kayak.com)
7. Agoda (www.agoda.com)
8. Hotels.com (www.hotels.com)
9. GetYourGuide (www.getyourguide.com)
10. Travelocity (www.travelocity.com)

These websites provide a variety of options for reserving excursions, events, and lodging in a number of locations, including Tahiti and Bora Bora. Before making a reservation, make careful to shop about, read reviews, and look into any special conditions.

Navigational apps that are essential

The following are some crucial navigational apps:

1. Google Maps: Google Maps is a well-liked and trustworthy navigation program that offers

thorough maps, step-by-step instructions, real-time traffic updates, and information on public transportation.

2. Waze: Waze is a crowdsourced navigation program that provides real-time traffic reports, suggested routes, and notifications about accidents, road dangers, and police activity. It's especially helpful for avoiding gridlock in the streets.

3. Apple Maps: The navigation app for iOS devices by default is Apple Maps. It offers thorough maps, step-by-step instructions, up-to-the-minute traffic data, and choices for public transit.

4. MAPS.ME is an offline navigation program that enables you to download maps of particular regions or nations for usage when you don't have access to the internet. It provides thorough directions, maps, and points of interest.

5. Sygic: A navigation program that provides both online and offline maps is called Sygic. It offers real-time traffic updates, voice-guided turn-by-turn directions, speed limit details, and lane advice.

6. Click Here to Go Offline maps, turn-by-turn directions, information on public transportation, and real-time traffic updates are all provided by the navigation software WeGo. Additionally, it offers options for riding a bike, walking, and cycling.

7. Citymapper is a navigation tool made specifically for urban settings. In many major cities across the world, it offers information about public transportation, including as routes, timetables, and real-time updates for buses, trains, and other types of transportation.

8. Navmii: Navmii is a free navigation app that provides voice-guided instructions, offline maps, and current traffic data. A speed limit display and sites of interest are also included.

Keep in mind to drive safely and obey all local traffic laws and regulations when using these applications.

Scams to Avoid

Here are a few typical scams to be aware of and steer clear of:

1. Online Booking Scams: Use caution while making online reservations for lodging, travel, or activities. Before entering any personal or payment information, make sure the website or platform is legitimate. Rely only on trusted, well-known booking sites.

2. Fake Wi-Fi Networks: Refrain from connecting to untrusted or unknown Wi-Fi networks, particularly in public areas. Your personal information can be intercepted by scammers using bogus networks. For additional security when connecting to public Wi-Fi, use a virtual private network (VPN).

3. ATM skimming: Use ATMs with caution, particularly in tourist areas. As thieves may employ skimming devices to steal your card information, look out for any strange gadgets attached to the ATM. Use ATMs that are situated in safe and well-lit areas, and cover your hands when entering your PIN.

Use licensed taxis or reliable ride-sharing services to avoid taxi scams. Some cabbies may take longer journeys or trick the meter in order to overcharge gullible visitors. Before beginning the journey, decide on the fare or take a metered cab.

5. Street Scams: Watch out for typical street scams including pickpocketing, diversions, and people who offer unasked-for assistance. Keep an eye on your surroundings, be cautious with your possessions, and refrain from flashing anything of value.

6. Fake Officials: Be on the lookout for anyone who are impersonating police officers or other officials. Tourists may be targeted by scammers who attempt to extort money or personal data. Ask for correct identification, and if you have any questions, get in touch with the local authorities or visit a nearby tourist information center.

7. When attending timeshare seminars, proceed with caution. Some presentations might use high-pressure sales techniques or include unstated fees. Before making any decisions, thoroughly read any contracts and take your time.

8. Charity Scams: Exercise caution when speaking with anyone who claim to be from philanthropic organizations. Before donating money or giving personal information, be sure they are legitimate. If you want to help, make a direct donation to a trustworthy charity.

Don't forget to follow your gut, do your homework before traveling, and keep up with local scams while you're there. Maintain vigilance and caution, and it's advisable to err on the side of caution if anything seems off.

Facts about Bora Bora and Tahiti

The following information relates to Tahiti and Bora Bora:

Tahiti: 1. Tahiti, which is situated in the South Pacific Ocean, is the biggest island in French Polynesia.
2. It is a part of the French Polynesian archipelago known as the Society Islands.
3. Papeete, the nation of Tahiti's capital, serves as the primary airport for international travel.
4. Tahiti is renowned for its breathtakingly beautiful landscape, which includes verdant highlands, blue lagoons, and magnificent beaches.

5. The island has a thriving culture that features age-old dance, music, and handicrafts.

6. English is frequently spoken in tourist areas of Tahiti, but French and Tahitian are the official languages.

7. Tahiti is a well-liked location for water sports like surfing, scuba diving, and snorkeling.

8. A variety of bird species, marine life, and tropical vegetation can be found on the island.

9. Tahiti has a tropical climate with moderate temperatures all year long. The wettest months are typically November through April.

1. Bora Bora is a little island that is a part of the Society Islands and is situated in French Polynesia.

2. It is renowned for its spectacular beauty and is frequently referred to as the "Pearl of the Pacific" or the "Romantic Island."

3. Bora Bora is renowned for its gorgeous overwater bungalows and blue lagoon, which is perfectly pure.

4. Mount Otemanu, an extinct volcano that rises from the island's center, is a recognizable feature of Bora Bora.

5. The island is a well-liked honeymoon and opulent holiday spot that draws tourists from all over the world.

6. Bora Bora provides a range of water sports, such as sailing, jet skiing, snorkeling, and diving.

7. Polynesian traditions and rituals have an impact on the local Bora Bora culture, with dancing and music playing a major part.

8. French and Tahitian are the official languages of Bora Bora, while English is also frequently used in tourist areas.

9. Bora Bora endures a dry season from May to October and has a tropical environment with mild temperatures all year round.

Both Tahiti and Bora Bora are renowned for their unmatched natural beauty, welcoming people, and the chance to visit a tropical paradise in the middle of the South Pacific.

Do's and Don'ts

When traveling to Tahiti and Bora Bora, keep the following in mind:

1. Respect the norms and culture of the area. Learn a few simple words in French or Tahitian to express your gratitude.
2. Engage in customary pursuits and experiences, such as watching a Tahitian dance show or dining on regional fare.
3. Preserve and safeguard the natural world. Avoid causing harm to other natural resources or coral reefs by properly disposing of your waste.
4. To protect oneself from the potent tropical sun, drink plenty of water and wear sunscreen.
5. Engage in activities like snorkeling, diving, hiking, or taking a boat tour to explore the natural beauty of the islands.
6. Sample some of the regional cuisine, which frequently consists of tropical fruits, fresh seafood, and age-old specialties like roast

suckling pig and poisson cru (marinated raw fish).

7. When visiting local towns or holy places, dress modestly and cover yourself when necessary, especially in traditional or religious settings.

8. Be mindful of private property, and ask permission before accessing any locations that are off-limits.

Don'ts:

1. Don't leave trash or other litter behind. Maintain cleanliness on the islands and use proper garbage disposal.

2. Steer clear of coral reefs and their inhabitants. They must be protected since they are delicate ecosystems.

3. Refrain from taking items from the beaches or other natural areas, such as shells or sand.

4. Refrain from excessive public shows of affection because they might not be acceptable in some cultural circumstances.

5. To prevent unintentional harm, avoid swimming or snorkeling too closely to coral reefs.

6. Avoid feeding or interfering with wildlife, as this can upset their normal behavior and the ecosystem's equilibrium.

7. Avoid engaging in unlawful activities, such as the possession or use of drugs that are forbidden.

8. Refrain from excessive alcohol consumption and always drink sensibly.

You may ensure a polite and pleasurable trip to Tahiti and Bora Bora by adhering to these dos and don'ts while also helping to preserve their natural beauty and cultural legacy.

Phrases

Tahitian and French are the primary languages used in Tahiti and Bora Bora. These words and phrases are useful in both languages:

Ia ora na is the Tahitian word for "hello," and it is pronounced "ee-ah oh-rah-nah."

2. I'm grateful, Mauruuru (pronounced mah-roo-roo).

3. Farewell, Nana (pronunciation: nah-nah)

4. The letter E in the word "yes"

5. No-Aita (pronounce it as eye-tah)

6. Kindly - Muruuru (pronounce it mah-roo-roo).

7. Excuse me, Tia ia outou (pronunciation: tee ah ee ah oh too)

8. "I'm sorry," pronounced "E muruuru" (ay mah-roo-roo).

9. What's up? Pehea oe? (pronunciation: peh-heh oh-eh)

10. Teie o'u i'a is my name; it is pronounced tay-ay oh-oo ee-ah.

1. Good morning - Bonjour (pronounce it bon-zhoor)

2. Merci, which is pronounced "mer-see,"

3. Au revoir, pronounced "oh ruh-vwah," means "goodbye."

4. Wee (pronounced wee) - Oui

5. Non (pronounced nohn)

6. S'il vous plaît, pronounced "seel voo play,"
7. Excuse me, excuse me, excuse me (pronounced ex-kewz-mwah)
8. I apologize - Je suis désolé (pronunciation: zhuh swee day-zoh-lay)
9. What's up? - How is it going? (pronunciation: koh-mah sah vah)
10. My name is (pronounce it zhuh mah-pehl) - Je m'appelle

When visiting Tahiti and Bora Bora, it's a good idea to pick up a few simple phrases in the native tongue. It demonstrates respect for the local way of life and can improve your ability to interact with the populace.

Insider tips

Here are some expert tips for traveling to Bora Bora and Tahiti:

1. Schedule ample Time: Allow yourself ample time to take full use of the islands. Tahiti and

Bora Bora have a lot to offer, from taking in the breathtaking scenery to participating in a variety of water sports. Consider your agenda carefully and try not to rush through your visit.

2. Take into account island hopping: While Bora Bora is a well-liked vacation spot, take into account visiting other islands in French Polynesia as well. Every island has a distinct charm and charms of its own. To experience the various facets of the area, take into consideration traveling to Moorea, Huahine, or Raiatea.

3. Embrace the Local Culture: Seize the chance to fully engage with the community. Attend traditional dance performances, explore neighborhood markets, sample regional cuisine, and converse with the welcoming residents. Your overall experience will be improved by learning about the cultural heritage.

4. Respect for the environment and wildlife: Bora Bora and Tahiti are well known for their pristine marine habitats and environs. By

eliminating littering, avoiding harm to coral reefs, and practicing responsible tourism, you may show that you respect the environment. Participate in environmentally responsible pursuits and aid regional conservation initiatives.

5. Travel Outside the Resorts: While the resorts in Bora Bora are luxurious and provide breathtaking vistas, you shouldn't restrict yourself to staying there. Explore the nearby communities, undiscovered beaches, and undiscovered tourist sites. This will enable you to see the islands for what they truly are.

6. Budget Your Money: French Polynesia, which includes Tahiti and Bora Bora, may be a pricey travel destination. Be prepared to pay more for lodging, meals, and activities. Plan your spending wisely and look into inexpensive options, such local restaurants or guesthouses.

7. Pack appropriately: Bring light, breathable clothing that is appropriate for a tropical climate. Don't forget to pack the necessities for

exploring, including sunscreen, insect repellant, a cap, and comfortable shoes. Consider carrying snorkeling equipment or water shoes if you intend to participate in water sports.

8. Accept a Slower Pace: French Polynesia works on "island time," which is a slower pace. Accept the slower tempo, take your time, and savor the relaxed environment. To really unwind and take in the splendor of the islands, avoid rushing through your activities.

You'll be better equipped to make the most of your trip to Tahiti and Bora Bora by keeping these insider recommendations in mind, ensuring a memorable and pleasurable experience.

Cost of travel

The cost of traveling to Tahiti and Bora Bora might change depending on a number of variables, such as the season, your travel preferences, your hotel preferences, your food selections, and the activities you intend to partake in. Here are a few general cost factors to think about:

1. Flights: Depending on your point of departure, the season, and the airline you choose, the cost of flights to Tahiti and Bora Bora might vary dramatically. During the busiest travel times, prices typically increase. To get the greatest discounts, it is important to book your flights far in advance.

2. Lodging: Tahiti and Bora Bora provide a variety of lodging alternatives, including five-star resorts, guesthouses, and vacation rentals. Depending on the amount of luxury and location, prices can vary significantly. Popular in Bora Bora, overwater bungalows are generally more pricey than other types of lodging.

3. Dining: Tahiti and Bora Bora provide a variety of dining alternatives, from luxury restaurants to small, neighborhood cafes and food trucks. Depending on the sort of institution

you visit, meal prices can change. Consider visiting neighborhood markets and sampling the reasonably priced local cuisine if you're on a tight budget.

4. Recreational opportunities: Tahiti and Bora Bora provide a variety of recreational opportunities, including water sports, island tours, cultural encounters, and spa services. Researching and comparing pricing in advance is advised because activity prices can change. While some activities might be included in resort packages, some might have additional costs.

5. Transportation: Depending on the form of transportation, transportation prices within the islands can vary. There will be fees for taxis, rentals, and guided tours. Flights between islands or ferry rides between islands could potentially cost money.

In order to make sure that your travel expenses are within your means of support, it is crucial to plan and budget appropriately. Budgeting can be made easier by doing price comparisons, planning ahead, and taking into account more affordable options like guesthouses or self-catering lodging.

Money Saving Advice

Here are some suggestions for how to travel to Tahiti and Bora Bora while saving money:

1. Consider traveling during the shoulder seasons or low season, when rates for lodging, activities, and flights are often more affordable. Avoiding busy travel times can help you get better discounts and deals.

2. Plan and Reserve Early: Plan and reserve your travel, lodging, and activities well in advance. This enables you to benefit from early bird pricing and exclusive offers.

3. Investigate Alternative Accommodations: Look beyond opulent resorts and take into account other lodging options like guesthouses,

vacation rentals, or smaller hotels. These choices are frequently more affordable and could offer a more genuine local experience.

4. Self-Catering: If you're living in a place with a kitchen, think about cooking part of your meals rather than eating out every time. Visit your neighborhood markets to buy groceries and fresh vegetables to reduce the cost of your meals.

5. Consume like a Local: Look for inexpensive and delectable meals at nearby restaurants, food trucks, and marketplaces. When compared to posh restaurants, these locations frequently provide real cuisine at reduced pricing.

6. Don't Eat Too Much at Resorts: While it's fun to try out resort restaurants, keep in mind that these meals can be more pricey. Think of taking advantage of one or two exceptional resort dinners while spending the remainder of your trip exploring other nearby options.

7. Bring Snacks and Water: Stay hydrated and fed during the day by bringing snacks and refillable water bottles. By doing this, you can avoid spending a lot of money on drinks and snacks while you're out and about.

8. Research Free and Low-Cost Activities: Look for activities that are free or inexpensive that are offered on the islands. Discover free public attractions including beaches, hiking trails, cultural events, and neighborhood fairs for a genuine experience without breaking the bank.

9. Take Public Transportation: If possible, choose shared shuttles or public transportation over taxis or private transports. You may be able to reduce your transportation expenses by doing this, especially for local travel.

10. Utilize Included Amenities: If you're staying at a resort, find out what amenities and activities are included. Some resorts include free use of snorkeling gear, water sports equipment, and cultural programs in the cost of the stay.

You can reduce the cost of your trip to Tahiti and Bora Bora without sacrificing the experience and pleasure of the lovely islands by using these cost-cutting suggestions.

Packing guides

For a trip to Tahiti and Bora Bora, you should think about carrying the following items:

1. Swimsuits or swim trunks are appropriate for warm tropical conditions. Lightweight and breathable apparel is also recommended.
- Sarongs or cover-ups for the beach
- Comfy sandals or walking shoes
- Hat or cap for sun protection - Light jacket or sweater for cooler evenings or air-conditioned settings - Flip-flops or waterproof sandals for the beach and water activities
- An umbrella or raincoat, especially if you're going during the rainy season

2. Beach equipment: a beach mat or towel
- Snorkeling equipment (if you own it; on the islands, it is frequently available for rental)
Reef-safe sunscreen
- Eyewear
- A visor or sunhat
- A phone cover or bag that is waterproof
- A backpack or beach bag for your essentials

3. Travel paperwork and necessities:
- A current passport (valid for at least six months after the date of entry).
- Information on travel insurance
- E-tickets or tickets for flights
- Reservations made for lodging
- Cash in the country or credit cards
- Travel adapters for electrical outlets (Type E and Type F sockets are used in French Polynesia).

4. Individual Items:
- Personal care items including shampoo, toothpaste, and toothbrushes
- Prescription drugs, if necessary

- Insect repellant - A basic first aid kit with bandages and painkillers
- Items for personal hygiene

5. Electronics, including a cellphone and charger
- If desired, a camera or underwater camera
- Portable chargers or power banks
- An all-purpose power adaptor, if necessary
- A phone case that is waterproof or water-resistant

6. Additional:
- Maps or travel guides
- Snacks and a reusable bottle of water
- A travel lock to keep your belongings secure.
– A money belt or pouch to protect valuables
- A portable umbrella providing protection from the sun or the rain.
- Any unique goods you may need, such as contact lenses or prescription glasses

Prior to packing, be sure to review the airline's luggage policies and weight restrictions to guarantee compliance. Additionally, take into account the specific activities you intend to partake in and pack appropriately (e.g., hiking boots for hiking, workout attire for fitness activities).

Always try to pack lightly and allow room in your bag for any mementos or other items you might wish to bring home from your vacation.

Travel Insurance

Travel insurance is a crucial component of travel preparation since it offers financial security and peace of mind in the event of unforeseen circumstances or emergencies. It is essential to think about getting travel insurance that covers the following situations when visiting Tahiti and Bora Bora:

1. vacation Cancellation or Interruption: If your vacation is canceled or interrupted for a covered reason, such as illness, injury, or unforeseen

circumstances, this coverage can reimburse you for non-refundable charges.

2. Medical Expenses: Verify that your travel insurance covers medical costs, including ambulance service, hospital stays, and, if required, medical evacuation. Having proper coverage is crucial because French Polynesia's medical expenses might be rather significant.

3. Lost or Delayed Baggage: This insurance can pay for lost, stolen, or damaged luggage and other personal items while you're traveling. If your baggage is delayed for a predetermined amount of time, it may also cover costs for necessities.

4. Travel Delays: If your flights or other means of transportation are significantly delayed, travel insurance may be able to help with additional costs like lodging, food, and transportation.

5. Emergency Support: Look for travel insurance that provides round-the-clock emergency

support. This can include aid finding medical facilities or setting up transportation, access to a helpline for medical emergencies, and travel suggestions.

6. Activities and Adventure Sports Coverage: Verify that your insurance coverage covers any planned adventurous activities, such as hiking, scuba diving, or snorkeling. Review the policy's specifics carefully since some activities can call for extra protection or have specific restrictions.

The terms and conditions of the travel insurance coverage, including any exclusions and limitations, should be carefully read and understood. Consider getting travel insurance as soon as you arrange your trip to assure coverage for any unanticipated events that might occur before or during your trip.

Check to see if you already have insurance through a credit card, your company, or personal insurance policies. It's critical to evaluate your requirements and pick a travel insurance plan that best meets them and offers sufficient coverage for your trip to Tahiti and Bora Bora.

Telecommunication

There are a few options accessible in Tahiti and Bora Bora for mobile connectivity and telephony, including eSIM options. Here is a summary:

1. Local SIM Cards: You can buy a local SIM card from several service providers when you arrive at the airport or in major towns. Having a local phone number and data plan for your trip is made possible by doing this. To use a local SIM card, you must have a GSM-compatible phone that is unlocked.

2. overseas Roaming: Ask your home mobile service provider about the alternatives and prices for overseas roaming. Although this might be a practical choice, keep in mind that roaming costs might be rather high. It is advised to carefully

evaluate the roaming rates and take other choices into consideration if the costs are too high.

3. Travelers can choose from eSIM choices from some cell service providers. Without a physical SIM card, you can remotely activate a plan with an eSIM. Find out from your cell service provider whether French Polynesia is covered by them and whether they provide eSIM services.

4. Wi-Fi and Internet connection are often available in Tahiti and Bora Bora's hotels, resorts, and cafes, though the quality and speed can vary. Major cities also have internet cafés where you can pay to use the internet.

It is advised to speak with your cell service provider in advance to learn more about the possibilities available for overseas travel, including options for Tahiti and Bora Bora. Inquire about their unique trip packages, eSIM availability, and international roaming pricing.

Research the regional mobile service providers and compare their plans to find the best prices and coverage if you intend to use a local SIM card or eSIM. To select the plan that best meets your needs, take into account variables like data allotments, call rates, and validity periods.

Don't forget to verify that your phone is compatible with the French Polynesian local network frequencies. Additionally, before buying and using a local SIM card or eSIM, make sure your phone is unlocked.

Always have a backup communication strategy in place, such as using offline maps or keeping a physical map on hand, in case your primary telecommunication option experiences any problems.

7-day each itinerary for Tahiti and Bora Bora

Sure! An example 7-day itinerary for Tahiti and Bora Bora is provided below:

7-Day Itinerary for Tahiti:

Day 1: Fly into Tahiti and take a taxi to your hotel.
- Unwind and get used to the island.
- Take a leisurely evening and explore the neighborhood.

Day 2: Go on an island trip with a guide in Tahiti, stopping at sites like Point Venus, Taharaa Viewpoint, and the Arahoho Blowhole.
- Shop for gifts and discover the local culture by going to the Papeete Market.
- Take a stroll in the evening in Papeete along the waterfront promenade.

Day 3: Spend the day in Moorea, a nearby island renowned for its breathtaking scenery.
- Take part in activities like hiking, snorkeling, or a trip to the Belvedere Lookout for sweeping vistas.
- In the evening, fly back to Tahiti and take it easy over supper.

Day 4: Take a tour of Tahiti's stunning black sand beaches, like Papenoo Beach and La Plage de Maui. To find out more about the past and present of French Polynesia, go to the Museum of Tahiti and Her Islands. Take a boat at dusk or eat dinner at a neighborhood eatery.

Day 5: Take part in water sports like kayaking, paddleboarding, or snorkeling in Tahiti's crystal-clear lagoons.
- - Take a stroll along the picturesque walking pathways in the lush tropical Vaipahi Gardens. - Pamper yourself with a relaxing traditional Polynesian spa treatment.

Day 6: Go on a 4x4 safari tour to see Tahiti's untamed interior, which features volcanic scenery and waterfalls. To find out more about the famed artist's relationship to Tahiti, go to the Paul Gauguin Museum. Enjoy a dinner entertainment and traditional Polynesian dance performance.

Day 7: Take a sunset cruise to take in the stunning vistas of Tahiti's coastline, or spend the day at leisure lounging on the beach or perusing the neighborhood cafes and stores.
- Travel to further French Polynesian islands or depart from Tahiti.

A 7-day itinerary for Bora Bora:

Day 1: Fly into Bora Bora and take a taxi to your hotel.
- As you settle in, take in the breathtaking views of the blue lagoon.
- At the pool or on the beach, unwind and unwind.

Day 2: Go snorkeling or scuba diving in the lagoon to discover the underwater world.

- Take a boat tour of the island to see the picturesque Mount Otemanu and the verdant surroundings.

- Have a special meal for two at one of the waterfront establishments.

Day 3: - Set off on a jet ski excursion to find the lagoon of Bora Bora's hidden treasures.

Visit the Coral Gardens to go snorkeling amidst colorful coral reefs and exotic species. Enjoy a picnic lunch while unwinding on a personal motu (islet).

Day 4: Take a helicopter tour to get a bird's-eye perspective of the beautiful scenery of Bora Bora.

- Take part in water sports like parasailing, paddleboarding, or kayaking.

- For the utmost in relaxation, treat yourself to a spa service or a couple's massage.

Day 5: Visit the Bora Bora Pearl Farm to learn about the unique pearl-growing process, and take a guided island tour to learn about the history and culture of the island. Take a sunset cruise or a trip in a traditional outrigger canoe.

Day 6: For sweeping vistas of the island, go on a trekking tour to Mount Pahia or Mount Otemanu.
- Explore the neighborhood of Vaitape and look around the local boutiques and shops for trinkets and crafts.
- Unwind on Matira Beach, one of Bora Bora's most stunning beaches. In the evening, take in a traditional Polynesian dance and fire spectacle.

Day 7: Spend the day at leisure, taking advantage of the resort's amenities or signing up for extracurricular activities like deep-sea fishing or a sailboat ride after dusk. Enjoy a goodbye meal and the last glimpses of Bora Bora's magnificent surroundings.

It's crucial to note that this is only a recommended schedule; you can change it to suit your tastes, your time constraints, and any particular activities or attractions you want to add. Additionally, bear in mind that some activities depend on the weather, so it's a good idea to prepare backup plans just in case.

Conclusion

Memorable Experiences in Tahiti and Bora Bora

The thrills and memories you will have from visiting Tahiti and Bora Bora will last a lifetime. These islands provide a paradise-like setting for relaxation and adventure, with their immaculate beaches, blue lagoons, and rich Polynesian culture. Tahiti and Bora Bora offer a variety of activities, whether you like to relax on the lovely beaches, climb through verdant mountains for spectacular vistas, or snorkel or dive to experience the vivid underwater environment.

Visit vibrant marketplaces, sample authentic Polynesian cuisine, and take in fascinating dance performances to fully experience the local culture. The majestic Mount Otemanu in Bora Bora and the verdant landscapes of Tahiti are only two examples of these islands' breathtaking natural splendor.

To truly experience the lagoons' pristine waters, be sure to take advantage of the water sports opportunities, which include kayaking, paddleboarding, and jet skiing. Enjoy the comfort of overwater bungalows, where you may awaken to breathtaking ocean views and experience the utmost in relaxation.

Tahiti and Bora Bora offer a magical location that will make treasured memories, whether you're looking for a romantic break, an adventure-filled holiday, or simply a peaceful escape. Your experience in Tahiti and Bora Bora will stay a priceless memory for years to come thanks to the friendliness of the locals, the incredible natural wonders, and the spectacular beauty of these islands.

.

Made in the USA
Thornton, CO
01/03/24 18:47:46

121fbb6a-1688-4e48-b22b-ddbdb8bc94e7R02